God Took My Clothes

A DISCUSSION OF GOD, LOVE, SPIRITUAL INSIGHTS, AND THE AFTERLIFE, BASED ON OVER 700 NEAR DEATH EXPERIENCES

DAVID SUICH

Published by Mindstir Media, LLC
45 Lafayette Rd | Suite 181| North Hampton, NH 03862 | USA
1.800.767.0531 | www.mindstirmedia.com

Printed in the United States of America
ISBN-13: 978-1-7367342-6-1

TABLE OF CONTENTS

Chapter 7

INTRODUCTION

MY JOURNEY

12 years ago, I was facing a crisis. I had completely lost faith in God and was sure that if he even existed, he wasn't interested in me because I wasn't a good person. That crisis ended when I heard the testimony of an atheist who died, was led towards a hellish place, but was rescued when he called out to Jesus for help.[1] For reasons that I only later came to understand, he ended up in the afterlife completely naked, although nobody seemed to notice or even care about his nudity. His amazing story started me on a 12-year learning experience during which time I heard the testimonies of over 700 people who died in various ways, were revived, and told their stories of what they saw on the other side. Most went to Heaven, some went to Hell, but all their experiences were incredible, shocking, and life changing.

I no longer have "faith" in God because that implies a belief in something unknown or unproven. I now know as a basic fact of life that God and Heaven exist. The testimonies changed my entire life—my relationship with my friends and family, my attitude towards others, my political views, my career, and my attitude towards nature and the environment. The testimonies also gave me a wonderful knowledge of human immortality. This book is a summary of what I learned from those who have died, seen the afterlife, and returned.

A NON-DENOMINATIONAL BOOK

Although this book does occasionally mention Jesus and contains a few Bible quotations, this is definitely not a Christian book. The hundreds of testimonies that I have heard paint a clear picture of who God is and the meaning of our lives here on Earth. The testimonies indicate that God does not discriminate based on religion or spiritual beliefs. The people who have gone to Heaven include Christians, Muslims, Hindus, Jews, Buddhists, Catholics, Baptists, agnostics, atheists, and every other spiritual belief system you can imagine. God loves everyone regardless of their beliefs and does not punish people or send them to Hell because they happen to have been born in a culture where they were taught the "wrong" religion or an inaccurate representation of God. No matter what you believe about God, even if you believe he does not exist, you are still loved just as much. God has no judgments about our judgments.

DISCLAIMER

I have done my best in this book to summarize the spiritual knowledge that I learned from near-death experiencers. Some insights are very clear and I have no doubt as to their accuracy, such as *The Main Point* described in the following pages. However, many things I discuss are not entirely clear from the testimonies, and I have made educated guesses based on partial information. I certainly do not want to discredit any religion by the ideas I present in this book, because all religions are doing the same thing that I am doing, which is speculating about God and spirituality. Within the existence of the physical realm, anything beyond speculation is nearly impossible. Religions may think they have all the answers, but they do not. Any talk about God, spirituality, and the afterlife is all guesswork. I have no doubt that I am mistaken about many concepts, so please do your best as you read this book to make your own judgments based on your own knowledge and experience, and listen to what your instinct tells you. Your heart is far more knowledgeable than any person's intellect, so listen to what rings true for you. Nobody really needs to worry too much about details. God is not going to punish anybody for getting spiritual details wrong. He is a very tenderhearted and gentle benevolent source of all life, and completely understands and expects that humans will make many mistakes along the way, as all of us here on Earth do on a regular basis.

THE MAIN POINT

The first near-death experience I ever heard profoundly changed the course of my life. The following is an excerpt from that testimony, which summarizes the most important concept the near-death experiencers bring us:

> We began to converse, and he [Jesus] was talking with me and telling me things, and he brought over some angels. And we went over my life from beginning to end. And what they wanted to show me in my life is what I had done right and what I had done wrong. And without going through my whole life story, it was real simple. When I had been a loving, kind person, considerate of other people, it made the angels happy, it made Jesus happy, and they let me know that it made God happy. And when I had been selfish and manipulative, it made the angels unhappy, it made Jesus unhappy, and they let me know that it made God unhappy. What they were trying to convey to me in a nutshell was, the whole purpose of my existence had been to love God and love

my neighbor as myself. That's why I had been created. That's what I was in this world to do and to learn.[2]

If you read this book no further than this paragraph, you know the most important thing near-death experiencers teach us—**IT'S ALL ABOUT LOVE.**

ABOUT THE BOOK

"The sheer volume of evidence for survival after death is so immense, that to ignore it is like standing at the foot of Mount Everest and insisting that you cannot see the mountain."

— Colin Wilson

This book focuses on the dying experience, the life review, the environments of both Heaven and Hell, and the many spiritual insights that near-death experiencers bring back with them. It will not focus on the complete stories of individual experiences, as there are already hundreds of books written that detail their testimonies. Nor will this book address, in depth, the validity of these near-death experiences. Any person with an open mind who listens to the testimonies of those who have seen the other side would have difficulty dismissing them as hallucinations or a trick of the dying brain. You can read the words on these pages attentively enough, but what they cannot convey are the expressions of sincerity on the faces of near-death experiencers as they recount their stories. A book cannot show the tears in the eyes of people as they describe the beauty and blissful joy of Heaven. Nor do printed words convey the frustration people have while trying to describe an experience that is completely ineffable to people who presently perceive life from the perspective of the physical realm. The experiences cannot be described in terms of human language and common experience.

ARE THE EXPERIENCES REAL?

> "There is a principle which is a bar against all information, which is proof against all arguments, and which cannot fail to keep a man in everlasting ignorance—that principle is contempt prior to investigation."
>
> — *Herbert Spencer*

Most people find it difficult to believe the stories that near-death experiencers tell, because the stories include ideas and concepts that are contrary to the ideology of their religion. It is far more emotionally comfortable to rationalize why the experiences must be false, rather than to face the possibility that what religion and culture teaches might be wrong. I can tell you from personal experience that to challenge your most deeply held beliefs is downright terrifying. But had I not done so, I would never have found the greater truth about God and the corresponding peace and joy it has brought to my life.

Some argue that near-death experiences are nothing more than hallucinations, but I have never met a single individual whose life was so profoundly changed by a mere hallucination. Near-death experiencers return to this Earth as entirely different people. They are more loving, less materialistic, and more focused on meaningful relationships and serving humanity. Some return with enhanced empathic or psychic abilities. There has been more than one occasion where a person I interviewed told me secrets about myself I have never revealed to anybody.

As my investigations became more in depth, the evidence became irrefutable. Near-death experiencers recount conversations in other parts of the hospital that occurred while they were clinically dead. People blind from birth describe seeing for the first time and can describe the colors of the hospital rooms and workers' clothing.

Young children meet great grandparents in Heaven, and then later identify them, but only from pictures of when their great grandparents were young. Old age seems non-existent in Heaven. Some people meet a sibling in Heaven they never knew they had. Upon returning to Earth and questioning their parents, they find that either their parents had a child that died at birth or that their mother had a miscarriage.

The very notion that these hallucinations are a trick of the dying brain is nonsensical. Nevertheless, some people will not recognize their own immortality. As it is with many of mankind's greatest discoveries, when an incredible theory is first proposed, it is typically not met with open-minded consideration, but with profound skepticism and ridicule. Five hundred years ago, everyone—from the most educated scholars to the poorest peasants, was aware of one fundamental truth: The Earth was the center of the universe, and the sun and stars revolved around us. Then Nicolaus Copernicus, in his book *"On the Revolution of the Celestial Spheres,"* suggested the absurd. The Earth was not the center of the universe, but instead was traveling through space around the sun at 67,000 miles per hour. This notion was so preposterous and offensive to the populace at large that the Catholic Church condemned his book as heresy. Copernicus was forced to delay the publishing of his book until after his death to avoid the political and social firestorm it would have created. Although the idea seems unbelievable today, humanity will someday soon realize that many people on this planet have visited Heaven, there is an all powerful and loving creator, and we, his children, are all immortal.

CHAPTER 1

DYING

"I think death is an illusion… I don't see any truth in the word death at all." [3]

— *Pam Reynolds, brain aneurysm*

WAKING UP

They died in various ways—car accidents, surgeries gone wrong, heart attacks, etc. There were less common deaths, including shootings, plane crashes, suicides, stabbings, drug overdoses, drownings, and even a few who were struck by lightning.

Death is not the end; it is only walking out of the physical form and into a freer life in the spirit realm, which is our true home. When we die and our spirit leaves our body and we find ourselves in our spiritual body in the spiritual world, we are the exact opposite of a ghost. People report feeling more alive and more real than they ever did in the physical realm. It is almost like waking up from a dream. When you are dreaming, you believe that your dream world is real. It is only when you wake up that you realize how unreal your dream was. If you can imagine going from a dream state to a waking state, and what kind of reality change that represents, just imagine taking one step further towards a higher level of consciousness and awareness. The physical world, this life, is the paper Mache world that has no real substance in comparison to the spirit world.

> "What it felt like was waking up, as if this existence here on this Earth was just a dream that I had. And I was waking up, and I was more alive and alert than I had ever been in my life."

> — *Kelli, pain medication overdose*

Even with such a difference in perception, many people do not immediately realize they are dead. They often see themselves lying in a hospital bed or at the scene of an accident, and some people fail to recognize their own body. Many of them say that all throughout life we see ourselves in only two dimensions, such as in a mirror, a photograph, or on a TV screen. For this reason, people often fail to recognize themselves when they see their own body for the first time from a three-dimensional perspective.

Other people seem to be very aware of the moment their spirit leaves their body, especially in cases of a slow death from prolonged illness. They report their spirit coming out of their body through their head or chest area, often reporting a feeling in their limbs of a bone-chilling cold more intense than any cold they have ever experienced. The cold usually begins at their feet and creeps up through their upper body. Those who were physically suffering are very relieved to rid themselves of their ailing bodies. They find themselves instantaneously pain free and are overjoyed to be young and healthy again. Others describe the sensation of leaving their physical bodies as a liberating feeling, like taking off an old, heavy, restrictive winter coat.

In some cases that would otherwise cause severe trauma, such as dying in a horrible accident or burning to death in a fire, the spirit leaves or is removed from the body just prior to the moment of death. In these cases, it is common that the person reports an angel or spiritual entity being the instrument of early removal from the body.

Some people try communicating with those in the physical world, wanting to reassure their loved ones they are alive and well and not to worry. But they soon discover that no one can hear or see them. This is not because they lack substance, but rather that we in the physical world have a veil that prevents us from seeing into the spiritual world. People who have undergone near-death experiences also report having super-senses. They can see through walls, hear the thoughts and feel the emotions of people around them, and they can pass through solid objects and float through the air with ease.

It is common for people who die during surgery to be able to look down at their own body and observe the operation in progress. As they hear the thoughts and feel the emotions of the surgeons and nurses who are usually in a state of panic and stress, the near-death experiencer is typically calm and often does not understand why everyone is so upset.

THE TUNNEL AND THE LIGHT

> But I felt something, and I heard some noise in the back, and I turned around to see what it was. There was a light. There was this little white light out there, and I was going towards it, or it was coming towards me, I don't know which. But we were getting closer. I could hear people singing, and this light kept getting closer, and it was warm. I don't know how to describe it [Tom begins to cry at this point]. But it's a warmth that just engulfs you. It's a light of such peace and such love. And as you get closer, it just wraps all the way around you. It just

felt like somebody's arms were around me just holding me. Everything about it was just so perfect.

— Tom, cancer surgery

Each near-death experience is uniquely different because Heaven creates an environment to make the individual feel comfortable. For example, a person who is unusually fond of nature might be brought into one of Heaven's amazingly beautiful gardens. Others are greeted or guided by loved ones who died before them.

Angels have been known to appear to people in the form of a classic angel with wings and a halo, such as you would see in a religious painting, but they do this only for our benefit to make the person feel comfortable. To others who have no preconception of what angels look like, they often appear in their natural form as beautiful radiant beings of light and love. There are even cases where angels appeared in their natural form, and then asked the individual if they would feel more comfortable with a different appearance. The incredible lengths that those in Heaven go through just to make us feel at ease are heartwarming and touching. But even with the variety of atmospheres and scenarios that those in Heaven create for us, many near-death experiences have common elements.

The length of each experience can vary considerably, with the shortest ones consisting of a person coming out of their body, observing themselves from above, and then being drawn back into their body as they are revived. Other near-death experiences involve extensive visits to Heaven or awful experiences in Hell that seem to last for an eternity. Several people were taken on tours of the universe, and one woman was even taken back to the beginning of time before the universe was created. For those who go to Heaven, the experience can begin in a dark and peaceful place, and at some point they notice a light, usually just a pinpoint at first. Some people are alone, while others are met by a loved one or spiritual being to travel with them through the dark tunnel towards the light. The person is drawn towards the light like a magnet and moves very fast, many describing their speed as "faster than light." When they arrive in the light, they describe the light as being 10,000 times brighter than the sun, but not at all painful or harmful to the eyes as it would be on Earth.

Being in this light, they report a feeling of love so powerful and so profound that even the word love is completely inadequate to describe it. One person said, "Imagine the 100 happiest moments of your life, put them all into one instant, and you still don't come close." Another person said, "Think of the most powerful love you have ever experienced on Earth, and multiply it by 500 times, and that is about what it feels like." When near-death experiencers recount being in God's light and feeling the profound ecstasy of his love, many begin to cry—even battle-hardened soldiers. God's beautiful presence is best described by the words of those who have experienced it:

> I'm standing in the very presence of almighty God. Instantly I knew I would never die for eternity. I was more alive than anybody can imagine. This was the height of the experience of life, filled up with life. And somehow I knew that this being was going to take care of me for eternity. It's the most joyful, most blissful experience you could ever have.
>
> *— Mickey, plane crash*

> The light is so warm and so glowing and so forgiving. The light had no judgment. There was no condemnation. There was no blaming, no shame. There was nothing but love and acceptance. The light knew everything I ever thought, did, and will do. The light knew me and called me by my name… The light said to me, "Andy, we love you." In back of the light were billions and billions of

other lights, and they all knew me. And they all said in a giant chorus, "Welcome home Andy." And I said out loud, "I'm home. At last, I'm home."

— Andy, drowning

And as the light approached, I realized that this was God. I didn't have to be told because it was like the universe reverberated his name. And then he said, "You can't take your life [through suicide]. It's not yours to take. Life is supposed to be hard. You have to pass through these difficulties." As he spoke to me, I was filled with understanding about the purpose of life and what we were doing here, and how important it is to think about how you treat other people. I could feel an incredible love and peace and compassion coming from him, and pain as well. I knew this was for what I had done.

— Angie, pill overdose and wrists slashed

And there before me was the living presence of the being of light. This being was all-knowing. It knew everything that was going to happen, and will happen, and the reasons behind them. There was a perfect justice. It contained all things that ever were, are, or will be, and it was loving me. It was pouring out this unconditional love at me. I figured this had to be God, because this was just beyond words and perfect in every possible sense.

— Beverly, motorcycle accident

This light surrounded me and took care of me, and I have never felt so good and so safe in all my life.

— Charles, heart attack

I came into this place of the most bright, beautiful, brilliant light conceivable. This light was so brilliant that it became a part of me, and I became a part of it. And I knew that I was safe.

— Dannion, struck by lightning

They took me down this exceptionally beautiful path, and it was brilliant. And they were taking me toward this great area that was not only exploding with beauty and color, but it was exploding with this absolute love of God that was beyond anything that I could ever describe or ever truly explain. I could hardly wait. I was absolutely overwhelmed by this sensation of being home, of being where I belonged.

— Mary, drowning

I suddenly became aware of the feeling of absolute love and absolute peace. It was like falling into a river of pure positive energy. There is nothing that I have ever experienced in this world that is even close to that. And I felt this absolute love, which was the most amazing experience I've ever had in my life.

— Tony, struck by lightning

There is more love than you can imagine. The feeling of how much love there is was incredible. The peace you have is a perfect peace. The only thing I can relate it to is when I was young, I would crawl on my mother's lap and she would cradle me and hold me and rock me. And that was the most peaceful, safe, and loving place. And you could multiply that feeling by 1000, and you still wouldn't come close to what it really feels like when you are there.

— Fred, heart attack

Quietly but steadily, a white light got closer and closer

until I was surrounded and almost wrapped up, like going into a hot bathtub after being chilled to the bone in the cold. I was in a loving presence; a white light that just filled me with a sense of peace and a kind of safe loving presence that is impossible to describe, but so wonderful that I can't stop trying to find words for it.

— Anonymous, car accident

The very first thing that came over me was this absolutely profound sensation of love. It was so unconditional, like the love of a child or the love of a mother for her child—the two of those interacting. And that love was so totally unconditional that it was overwhelming to me. It was beautiful and wonderfully accepting. And as I proceeded into this sense of very profound love, it was followed by a sense of purposefulness, that whatever is happening has a point to it. When I came back, my heart was filled with a sensation of being on fire with love.

— Gordon, severe pneumonia

The feeling that I had when I got there was that of warmth and comfort and peace. It was as if I had been an Eskimo all my life in the bone chilling cold and had never been warm, but occasionally got flashes of heat by standing next to an open fire. And all of a sudden, I was transported to a tropical island where it was nice and warm.

— Anonymous, heart failure

I moved into this tunnel of light. When I got out to the other side, it was only what I can describe as pure love—absolute pure peace. I wasn't even bothered about what I left behind, and eventually I met the only thing I can describe as pure perfection. I cannot describe it in any other way. And at that point I thought, I don't think I should be here, because I didn't really think that I was worthy to be in front of what was pure perfection.

— Heather, pregnancy complications

And at the end of this tube was the most beautiful set of lights… I was going to this light, and I just wanted desperately to go to this light because it was wonderful. It was peaceful. It was serene. It was everything you wanted life to be.

— Janet, blood clots in lungs after surgery

I watched as a wave of radiance came up. As this wave of light came off the source, it touched me, and I felt warmth and comfort. All the fear and darkness just seemed to go out of me, and I felt a living light flow through me. Shafts of radiance came out from the central core—it was like a white fire. There was phenomenal radiance in the central core. From that I watched this brilliant light piercing out, and I thought, even the stars in the universe, even the constellations must find their energy source from this focal point. A voice spoke to me from the center of the light. And he said to me, "Ian, do you wish to return? If you wish to return, you must see in a new light." I watched a wave of radiance come off him. It moved through me and all I got was love. The love was causing me to literally blubber. I was bawling my eyes out. And then, I could feel an acceptance coming.

— Ian, jellyfish stings

Everything became brilliant white light. This brilliant white light was not just light, it was also love. I began to feel very blissful, very exalted. It was an incredible feeling of having been loved in a way that I didn't even know love could be—just cradled and totally safe. I knew there wasn't anything that could ever harm me. I just knew that all was well, and everything was wonderful. I immediately knew that there was a perfect plan. I didn't have to worry about anything. All the things that we don't understand, it's all right. We don't have to. I remember the phrase, "The plan is perfect, and it is working itself out in its perfection." And after that, I just existed in this tremendous state of joy and ecstasy. And the ecstasy just built and built until it reached an ecstatic peak, and I thought to myself, how much more of this can I take before I shatter?

— Jayne, death during childbirth

Then I was surrounded by light so intense I could feel it. It just sort of permeated me. I felt this enormous love and well-being—peace if you will. I had some sense of omniscience or knowing everything. I felt that everything was right as it should be. There was a purpose to everything. I felt knowledge and glimpsed godhood... There was absolute understanding, absolute love, and absolute peace.

— Anonymous, car accident

It is the most important, stunningly exquisite event in my life. Basking in the light, experiencing our creator's love, power, and majesty are beyond description. Divine ecstasy and intoxication is about as close as I can begin to translate this into human words.[4]

— Book "Crossing Over and Coming Home"

I saw a very bright light and I was flooded by light. I felt so comfortable and I didn't want to leave. And I asked for a reason why I should go back. Why do I have to go back there? Then this being, this thing became very forceful and told me, showed me, that I still have a task to do, that I can't come home now.

— Robert, electrocution

Up there, there is a feeling of unbelievable mutual love. I have never experienced this feeling since, but I still long for it. If you made me choose, even if my life here [on Earth] was really good and I had everything I could wish for, I would still without hesitation choose the other side just for that feeling again.

— Evet, heart attack

I was immediately in this beautiful bright white light. It was a total immersion in light, brightness, warmth, peace, and security. It's difficult to describe. As a matter of fact, it's impossible to describe. Verbally it cannot be expressed. It is so intense that it is something that becomes you and you become it. I was peace. I was love. I was brightness. It was a part of me. Everything is a part of you, and it is just so beautiful.

— Joe, internal hemorrhaging after surgery

The only way I could describe my immediate feeling was, if you could see or feel a smile or complete contentment or happiness, that was it. It was the most wonderful time in my life. It was peaceful, quiet, and magnificent. It's hard to explain because it wasn't exactly worldly, so how can I use worldly words to explain it to you? All I can say is that it was a fantastic experience.

— Geraldine, pneumonia

Before me was this magnificent beautiful bright white light. I was confronted by true, pure love. This was perfection.

— Anonymous, car accident

As I got closer to the light, I had this very strong sense of "at last I'm home." I just dove right into it, into perfect love, peace, joy, and bliss—an amazing feeling!

— Rebecca, heart attack

I was in this place, but it wasn't a place like here on Earth. It was an environment or an atmosphere, and it was love. It was amazing. It was total bliss, total joy, total love, total acceptance, and a complete feeling that everything is fine, and always will be, and always has been. It felt like home. It felt like that is where I belonged, and that is the way it is supposed to feel all the time.

— Anonymous, car accident

And then there was light. And I was part of the light. And everyone that I had talked to, and been with during that time, was part of the light. And it was beautiful and full of joy, and there was no judgment. All there was, was love—beautiful, magnificent, all encompassing love.

— Sonia, car accident

A gleaming bright light will shine white from the heart of God with such power that you hardly dare to look into it and still won't be able to stare your eyes away from it.

— The Tibetan Book of the Dead,
written over 1200 years ago.

CLEANING UP

Fear, with all its negative emotional manifestations, does not exist in Heaven. It is created by the human brain and ego. As a result, there are no negative emotions in Heaven nor malice of any kind. Every person you meet in Heaven is far more trustworthy than your best friend or most trusted family member here on Earth. But here on this planet, there are financial scams, robberies, stabbings, shootings, murders, and a whole host of bad people that you need to protect yourself against. To survive in this dangerous world, you must learn to mistrust certain people and avoid being victimized. Some souls can become "darkened" by Earth's harsh environment, and for reasons that I do not fully understand, before a person is sent back to Earth, Heaven decides to put some people through a cleansing process that erases all the negativity and mistrust you learned during your earthly experiences. The process is simple. You stand in God's radiant presence, and tangible waves of his love, peace, wisdom, and compassion cleanse you. Hatred, strife, jealousy, anger, resentment, mistrust, racism, pain, pride, lust, envy, greed, competitiveness, and fear are all washed away—gone. Earth has no sorrow that Heaven cannot heal.

THE LIFE REVIEW

One of the first things that happens when you arrive in Heaven, and this is the only part of the experience that can be exceedingly unpleasant or even intolerable for some, is the life review. In the presence of God, Jesus, angels, and spiritual beings or any combination thereof, the floodlights are turned on. They have a record of everything you ever thought, said, did, and felt during your lifetime on Earth. There is absolutely no real privacy at all. There never has been since the beginning of time.

During this life review, they take you through your whole life from beginning to end, and you relive every significant moment. You re-experience things you thought, said, felt, and did, but with one important difference: In your earthly existence, you only experience life from the perspective of one person—you. But in your life review, you experience your life not only from your own perspective, but also simultaneously from the perspective of the people around you as if you were those people. You literally become every person that you have ever encountered, and you get to experience the direct result of your interactions with those people. And for better or worse, you experience whatever joy, happiness, peace, pleasure, pain, strife, frustration, humiliation, anxiety, fear, or any other emotion the people around you felt in reaction to what you did. The purpose of this life review is a learning experience. During the life review, you gain a great deal of knowledge and insight of how your behavior affected others and how they felt in reaction to the person you decided to be. This knowledge is a tremendous benefit in helping you to learn about loving others unconditionally and using your interactions to encourage and uplift your fellow man. It is an incredibly useful learning tool.

It is important to mention here that this is not like having to live an entire 80 years of your life over again. There is no time in Heaven or Hell, and near-death experiencers report the entire process as happening "very fast." Others describe it as having a panoramic review of their lives in three dimensions, where everything happens simultaneously. There is little focus at all on intention during this life review. For example, if you gave someone a compliment, but they misinterpreted it as an insult, you would still experience all the emotional pain they suffered because of their misinterpretation of what you said. If, while driving, you hesitate at a four-way stop to read a text message on your cell phone and another driver thinks you are being kind to let him go first, you will still experience the good feelings and gratitude toward the kindness he mistakenly believed you were showing him.

Some people also experience *The Ripple Effect.* Not only do you experience the effect you had on those directly around you, but you also feel how the change in their lives affected other people. For example, a man who bombs a city during a war could experience the pain and suffering of all the individuals who died in the explosions. He could feel the pain, anguish, and desperation that each wife feels when an army official knocks on the door and delivers the news that her husband was killed. He could experience the grief and sadness of each child who has lost their father and the negative effects it will have on the child's life.

One near-death experiencer who had been a bully during his lifetime relived an incident when he was driving his car and got into an altercation with a pedestrian who illegally crossed the street in front of him. He ended up in a fistfight with the pedestrian, beating the man up, and leaving him unconscious in the street. In his life review, he found himself right there in the same street again raining blows down upon his victim, but at the same time he experienced it from his victim's perspective. He felt every one of the 34 blows. He felt his nose break and his teeth breaking. He remembered waking up later, injured and filled with pain. He even experienced the embarrassment that his victim had about being beaten up in a fight.

Another man during his life review relived an incident when he was in grade school and made fun of an unpopular girl who was overweight and unattractive. He experienced how his insults affected her and made her a more reclusive person afterwards. He felt all the emotional pain he caused her. He remembered (as if he were her) going home to her parents and not wanting to talk about the incident, and just crying alone in her bed. He felt the distress of the parents and their feeling of helplessness—not knowing why their precious daughter was so sad and emotionally withdrawn.

You will also experience many things that you thought nothing of during your lifetime. One woman, during her life review, experienced an incident she had forgotten about where she was rushing to work one morning and stopped to give a stranded motorist a jump-start. She didn't even wait to be thanked and hurried off on her way to work. But during her life review, she experienced it from the perspective of the person who was stranded and beginning to feel desperate that no one was stopping to help her.

During their life reviews, many people experience the joy that just a small act of kindness can make in the life of another person. If you give a few dollars to a homeless man thinking nothing of it, you may discover in your life review that the man had not eaten for several days, and you will get to experience all the pleasure that the man felt in finally eating a good meal after being so desperately hungry.

One man who worked as a hospice employee helping terminally ill patients, was pleasantly surprised to experience the joy of each elderly person he was kind to during his career. He said that part of his life review felt like "emotional fireworks".

The life review extends to animals as well. During her life review, one woman who had lived on a farm when she was a child, experienced a time when she was washing a horse, but under the hot summer sun she got sleepy and left the horse covered in suds while she went off to take a nap. As the soap dried on the horse's skin, it became intolerably itchy. The woman experienced how miserable and angry the horse was at being left tied to a tree with no way to alleviate the itching and physical suffering.

Another person while going through his life review, was surprised to discover that one of the crowning achievements of his life was when he rescued a homeless cat that was on the brink of starvation. He took the cat into his home, nursed it back to health, and treated it as an adopted member of his family. It made such a difference in the cat's life! And yes, animals absolutely do have emotions.

During this life review, there is no judgment or anger from God or angels or any of the spiritual beings that are watching. Usually, the harshest judge is the person themselves, often feeling very guilty about the way they mistreated others. At some parts, the life review can become so unbearable that it must be stopped, and tangible feelings of love and acceptance are shined upon the person, until he or she calms down enough to continue the review.

As they take you through this review, when you cause another human being suffering, it is embarrassing to you and grieves those who are watching. You must understand that when you are in the presence of God, Jesus, or angelic beings, they make you feel as if you are the most important person in the whole world, and it's as if the entire universe was designed and functions just to make you the best possible expression of creation that you can be. They have such high hopes for us, so during the times in our lives when we are selfish or cruel to our fellow human beings, they are often disappointed, something like a very loving father would be upon watching his own son drop out of college and become a homeless drug addict. There is no anger or judgment, just sadness that the human did not chose the path of love.

Here are just a few of the lessons I learned from listening to people's life reviews:

> 1. Revenge is impossible. Whatever devious punishment or revenge I am planning for my intended victim, no matter how morally justified my revenge may be, I am going to have to suffer and feel that revenge myself someday. There are no winners with revenge. Everyone loses.
>
> 2. Always be kind and generous to others. It is quite impossible to help another human being without helping myself. Any kindness I show to others comes back to me.

3. Make good investments. $20 less money may not make much of a difference in my life, but it makes a huge difference in the life of a child in a third world country. I may never directly meet the child I help, but I will experience all the good that my financial support will make in his life.

4. Be conscious and considerate of others. It is quite easy to annoy or anger another person without even realizing it. I can't tell you how many times I found myself accidentally blocking somebody's path in the grocery store, or accidentally cutting off another driver I didn't see. I now realize I'm going to experience any frustration or anger I cause another person, even if it was unintentional. So now I try to be much more aware of the people around me.

5. When there is a problem, be calm and kind. I almost always get better results approaching a problem with kindness rather than anger. Keeping calm during a conflict is not only easier for the people I interact with, but it is also a lot easier for me.

6. Practice small random acts of kindness daily. There are small things I can do as I go through my day that don't cost me any time or money. These include things like saying "please" and "thank you," holding a door open for others, smiling at a child, or giving somebody a genuine compliment. It may feel awkward at first to say to a complete stranger, "That's a really sharp-looking suit" or "You have beautiful eyes." But in all the compliments I've given to strangers, I have never once received a negative reaction. And the beauty about giving compliments to strangers is that the awkwardness quickly fades, and it soon becomes second nature.

7. I try to cut others and myself lots of slack. I often remind myself of the words of a well-known cardiologist when he was interviewed and asked what we can do to take better care of our hearts. He said there are two principle rules. First, don't sweat the little things. Second, there are no big things. It is very easy for me, as a human being, to get frustrated with others and with myself when mistakes are made. But that's all part of being human. If I never made any mistakes, I'd have call myself "God" instead of by my given name. If I can learn to laugh at my own mistakes and be patient with the mistakes of others, it makes life a lot easier for everyone, especially me.

JUST AN AVERAGE GUY

An average guy? Well, there really is no such thing. Every person you meet is an amazing and powerful spiritual being temporarily inhabiting a human body. The young man who serves you coffee, your family members, your friends, your boss, the plumber who fixes your leaky faucet, the leader of your country, and the homeless guy asking you for spare change, all have one thing in common. They are ALL immortal. Not a single human being will ever die. Once a love-light being is created, that's it. It's permanent. It will always exist. YOU will always exist. But there is, however, a fate that seems worse than death.

CHAPTER 2

HELL

"Now there are people who talk about a light. There are people who talk about floating above. There are people who talk about a feeling of warmth and love. I didn't feel any of that. I felt NONE of that... I felt untold terror." [5]

— Dr. Donald Whitaker,
acute pancreatitis

If you are reading this book, it is highly unlikely you will ever end up in Hell. This is not to say that this book has any salvation value, but anyone who is seeking God will always receive a response from God in the form of tremendous help and guidance. The biblical principle of "seek and you shall find; knock and the door shall be opened" is a universal truth that is not limited to Christianity or people who believe in Jesus. Even the mere thought of wanting to become a better person starts an avalanche of assistance and guidance from those on the other side of the veil.

HELL IS REAL

Because their experiences were so positive, many near-death

experiencers who go to Heaven believe that there is no Hell, and everybody will go to Heaven when they die. But I believe this may be a false assumption on their part because they find it difficult to believe that such a loving God could allow a place like Hell to exist. I could not find a single instance of a near-death experiencer being directly told by God or anyone else in Heaven that there is no Hell. But I have encountered several near-death experiencers who went to Heaven and were either told something about Hell or were shown parts of Hell. For reasons unknown to me, only about 5% of the testimonies I have heard were hellish experiences.

WHO GOES TO HELL?

It was quite a shock to me to learn that God does not send anybody to Hell, and he is quite grieved when just one human being ends up there. Jesus specifically told one near-death experiencer that Hell was not meant for man. When a near-death experiencer begins telling their story, I can usually tell from the description of their lifestyle before their experience where they were going to end up. People who go to Hell are usually those who habitually create chaos and misery in the lives of others, or those who live entirely selfish lives, treating others with cruelty, contempt, or indifference. Children as defined by Mother Nature's standards (those who have not yet entered puberty) seem to be exempt from Hell. I have heard people speak about seeing children in Heaven, but I have never heard of a single sighting of a child in Hell. The youngest case I ever heard of a youth going to Hell was a 15-year-old girl who was living a selfish and chaotic lifestyle. She was involved in crime, drugs, and was living a narcissistic existence. And in the end, even she was given a second chance. I would not have heard her testimony otherwise.

Almost any major religion will tell you that if you don't join their religion and follow their rules, you will go to Hell. That idea is patently absurd. Those who go to Heaven or Hell often describe being attracted like a magnet towards their destination regardless of their religious choices on Earth. As near as I can tell, based on the way you lived your life and developed your soul, when you die you will be attracted to the place where there are souls like yours. If a person lives an entirely fear-based selfish life with all its negative manifestations, as their soul leaves their body, it may have the potential to be attracted to the place where there is nothing but fear—namely Hell.

The good news is that I have heard quite a few testimonies in which a person's spirit was being drawn towards Hell, and that person cried out to God for help and in EVERY such case was rescued. The Judeo-Christian doctrine that states it is too late to change your destiny after you die seems to be incorrect. I have even heard of a few rare testimonies of people who were in Hell and then were rescued after a change of heart or asking Heaven for help. Jesus told one man that he has rescued people from Hell.

LEVELS OF HELL

Hell is far worse than anybody is capable of imagining and is much worse than any description one might find in the Bible or any other religious book. It is designed to be so scary as to convince you to never go there. Just as there are levels of Heaven, there are different levels of Hell. But even the most benign level of Hell is pure torture. It consists of an empty void with no color, no light, no darkness, no walls, and no space—just absolute nothingness. The individual is in this empty world by themselves without a body (but no physical pain or discomfort) for what seems like an eternity with nothing other than their own thoughts and a completely perfect memory of their life on Earth. Even those who have been in this least torturous level of Hell described it as terrifying.

The following is a transcript of one near-death experiencer's testimony of his trip to this least torturous level of Hell:

> They say what happens in Vegas stays in Vegas. Well, in my case I don't want it to stay in Vegas, I want it to go around the world. I want people to know what happened to me because it was life changing for me. I was at a family reunion with my wife and we were going for a walk through the casino. After walking about 100 yards, I felt this circle of pain in my chest and I fell over dead.

> I woke up in this place that was all white. It wasn't light or dark, it was all white and I was wondering to myself, "Where am I at? What is this place?" I didn't see anything there and I wondered, "Where are the colors? What is this?" This wasn't a room. There were no contours there. There was no nothing there. I just kept wondering, "Where am I at?" And the next thing I know, I heard this voice say, "This is your eternity." And I thought to myself, "What?! This is my eternity? This can't be my eternity!"

> The next thing I knew, I woke up in the trauma unit. I opened my eyes and I saw the ceiling tiles. I thought to myself, "I'm back. I can't believe I'm back. How did I get back?" So, I closed my eyes and I said, "God, what do I have to do so I never go to that place again?" And you know, I heard a voice speak four words. And that voice said, "Get to know me." I asked that question because I didn't know the answer to the question, and I asked God. I didn't ask any doctor. There were no doctors around, no nurses, no nobody. I just want to let everybody know, that all I needed to do to avoid Hell and that terrible place I was in was to get to know God.

> — *David, heart attack*

THE DEPTHS OF HELL

> I began to hear people screaming and crying and groaning. I didn't know what that was. And then, as I began to see out of this thick smoke that was choking me, I was looking into what looked like the open mouth of a volcanic crater, a burning crater. And I was falling into this thing with no help. And worse than that, I began to see people in this fire. And they were screaming and crying, and they were burning, but they were not burning up.[6]

> *— Ronald, arterial bleeding*
> *during a street fight.*

I have decided to omit the horrific descriptions of Hell that I have heard from the near-death experiencers who have been there. But let me just say that whatever horrible fears people can create here on Earth (think about the absolute worst horror movies ever made), the collective group of souls in Hell can create scenarios that are far worse than any human being's worst nightmare.

If for whatever reason when you die you find yourself going towards a hellish place, my suggestion would be to call out to God for help. As stated before—in every case I have ever heard, when a person going towards Hell called out to God for help, they were rescued. The following example is one such testimony and is the source of this book's title. Howard Storm, an art professor, suffered a rupture in his lower duodenum, a critical portion of the digestive tract. He ended up naked and torn up just outside the gates of Hell until he cried out to Jesus for help. This is an edited version of his story from an interview he gave:

> I was a 38-year-old college professor, and I taught art, and I had taken a group of students and my wife, and we had gone around Europe. We had just done a three-

week tour, and this was the next to the last day. We were in Paris at 11 o'clock in the morning, when I had a perforation of my stomach. When this happened, the pain was the most acute pain I had ever experienced in my life, and it just dropped me right down to the ground.

And so, I was twisting, kicking, moaning, screaming, and yelling around on the floor, and my wife called the front desk, and they called an emergency service. A doctor came, and he called an ambulance because he knew what was wrong with me. They took me about eight miles across town to the public hospital, the General hospital in Paris, where I was taken into the emergency [room] and examined by two more doctors who knew exactly what was wrong with me. Then they took me away to the surgery hospital, a couple blocks away, and I was parked there because there wasn't any surgeon available to do the surgery. So, I laid there for eight hours in that hospital with no medication, no examination, no attention whatsoever, awaiting a surgeon to come to give me this operation that was critical.

It was now 8:30 at night. The nurse came in and said that they were very sorry, but they weren't able to get a doctor for me, and they would get one the next day. Well, when she said that, I knew that it was over for me. I knew that I was dead. The only thing that was keeping me alive was, I didn't want to die. I was scared to death of dying because as far as I knew, I was an atheist, a non-believer, a person who lived for the gratification they could get out of the moment. And dying to me, apart from the pain, was the worst thing that could happen because it was the end of life and there was no more. There wasn't anything else.

But when the nurse said that, the idea of trying to exist for another minute, another hour in this pain, it wasn't worth it anymore. I had been hanging on in the hopes that they would get a doctor, open me up, do the surgery, and fix the problem inside of me. But when they said they couldn't get a doctor, I said to my wife, "It's time for us to say goodbye, because I'm going to die now." And she got up and put her arms around me. I was lying in bed, and she told me how much she loved me, and I told her how much I loved her. This makes me really sad, and we made our goodbyes. We had been married 20 years, so we said all those kinds of things you say. I can't tell you because I will just start crying. She finally sat down because she knew it was over, and I knew too. It was just so hard looking at her crying like that, so I just closed my eyes and just let it go, and I went unconscious. I probably was unconscious for a very short while, a few minutes probably.

Suddenly, I was conscious again. I opened my eyes and looked, and I was standing up next to my bed. I knew exactly where I was, and what the situation was. There was no confusion in my mind. I felt more alive, more real than I have ever felt in my life. People ask me, "Were you a ghost?" I was just the opposite. I was very alive. As I looked around the room, I could see that there was something underneath the sheet on the bed—a body. And so, I bent over the bed (the head was turned away from me) and I looked at the face, and it looked like me. But that wasn't possible because I was standing there. I was alive. I was great! I mean, I was more than great.

I tried to talk to my wife, and she could not hear me or see me, but I thought that she was just ignoring me. I got very angry at her for ignoring me and for not paying attention to me. And I was screaming and yelling at her, "What's going on here? Why is this body in the bed that looks like me and how did it get there?" I had a sneaking suspicion that the body in the bed was me, but I did not want to think about that because that was too scary. I was getting really agitated and upset because this was all too weird. You know, this cannot be happening—it is impossible. I had a hospital gown on, and everything was very real.

Then, I heard people calling me outside of the room, and they were saying to me in soft, gentle voices, "Howard, you have to come with us now, come quickly, come out here." I went over to the doorway of the room, and there were people out in the hallway. The hallway was dank and gray. It was not light or dark—it was just gray. They were all in grayness, and there were men and women, and what they were wearing might possibly have been hospital uniforms. I asked them if they were from the doctor, to take me to the operation. I told them I was really sick, and I had to have an operation, and I was going to die if I didn't get this operation. I was supposed to have the operation eight hours ago. As I was telling them all this stuff, they were saying, "We know, we know, we understand, we have been waiting for you." I left the room, which was really clear and bright, and I went into the hallway which was dank and hazy, and I followed these people.

We had a very long journey. There was no time, and whenever I make a reference to time, it is just an illusion, because there was no time. But this journey, if I had to re-create it, I would have to walk from Nashville to Louisville [approximately 175 miles] or something, to re-create the walk with these people. As we walked, they stayed around me and kept moving me on, and it kept getting darker and darker. They were becoming more and more openly hostile to me. At first, they were sort of syrupy-sweet to get me to go with them, and then when I was going along with them, it was like, "Hurry up! Keep moving. Shut up. Stop asking questions." It started getting more ugly. And so, we got into complete darkness, and I was absolutely terrified. These people were very hostile. I didn't know where I was, so I said, "I am not going to go with you any further." They said, "You are almost there." And we started to fight. I was trying to get away from them, but they were pushing and pulling at me. There are now a lot of them. What originally had been a handful now was, since it was dark, hundreds or thousands—I have no idea. They were playing with me. Clearly, they could have just destroyed me if they wanted to. They did not want to destroy me. What they wanted to do was inflict pain on me because they derived… satisfaction out of the pain that I experienced.

What they were doing in the beginning part was, and it is really hard for me to talk about, so I am not going to tell you much about it, just a little bit, because it just gets too ugly. Initially they were tearing and biting, tearing with their fingernails, scratching, gouging, ripping, and biting. I was trying to defend myself. I tried to fight them off, tried to get away from them, but it was like being in a beehive. There were hundreds of them all over me. And I eventually was just lying on the ground there, all ripped up with pain everywhere, inside and outside. And even harder to bear than the physical pain was the emotional pain of what had just happened to me; the utter degradation that I had just experienced. I never once felt that it was unjust or wrong.

As I was laying there in the darkness, I heard my voice. It wasn't somebody else's voice. It wasn't the voice of God or anything. It was my voice. And I heard it speak, but I didn't speak it. Maybe it was the voice of my conscience. I don't know what it was. I distinctly heard my voice say, "Pray to God." I thought to myself, I don't believe in God. Pray to God? And I was thinking, even if I could pray, I don't know how to pray anymore. At that time, I hadn't prayed in 23 years. I was thinking when I was a child, and we said prayers in Sunday school, and we said prayers in church, what did we say? I was trying to think, because to me, to pray was to recite something that I had learned. That is what I thought a prayer was. I was saying, "The Lord is my shepherd, give us this day our daily bread, my country 'tis of thee… no, that's not a prayer, that's wrong. Let's see, yea though I walk through the valley of the shadow of death, four score and seven years ago our forefathers…" I was getting all of them mixed up, and I couldn't remember how to pray.

And then the people who were around me, every time I would mention God, these people who had attacked me and beaten me, it was as if mentioning God was like throwing boiling water on them. They would shriek. They would scream. They would yell in worse profanity than anything I have ever heard in this world. The other thing that was happening was, they couldn't bear to be around me talking about God. It was so painful for them to hear about God, that they kept backing away and backing away. I had a sense that I could push them away by talking about God. I was trying to remember prayers, and was getting all confused and mixed up, and it was just all crazy. And eventually as I was lying there, I realized that they were gone, and I was alone. I was alone there in that darkness for an eternity… There was absolutely no sense of time.

But I thought about my life. I thought about what I had done and what I hadn't done. I thought about the situation I was in. And the conclusion that I came to was, that during my adult life, I had lived an entirely selfish life. My only god in my adult life was myself. I realized that there was something terribly, terribly wrong with my life, and that the people who attacked me were the same kind of people I was. They were not monsters. They were not demons. They were people who had missed *it*. The point of being born and being alive in this world; they had missed it. And they had lived lives of selfishness and cruelty, and now were in a world where there was nothing else but selfishness and cruelty. And they were doomed to inflict that upon each other and upon themselves, probably forever and ever without end. And now I was a part of it. And although I didn't want to be there, it seemed like probably that was the right place for me to be. There was a sense of; this is what I deserve. This is what I lived. You can't imagine how emotionally painful that was.

And I'm lying there for time without end, thinking about my fate. In the back of my mind comes up an image of myself as a child, sitting in a Sunday school classroom, singing, "Jesus loves me." I could hear it in my mind, "Jesus loves me, this I know…" I recalled myself singing it, and I could hear myself as a child singing it. More important than anything else was that I could feel in my heart, that there was a time in my life when I was young and innocent, when I believed in something good, when I believed in something other than myself, when I believed in someone all good, all powerful, who really cared about me. I knew that I wanted that back, that which I had lost, that which I had thrown away, that I had betrayed. I wanted that back. I didn't know Jesus, but I wanted to know Jesus. I didn't know his love, but I wanted to know his love. I didn't know if he was real, but I wanted him to be real. Because I trusted that there was a time in my life that I had believed in something, and I had known once as a child that it was true, I wanted to trust that it was true.

So, I called out into the darkness, "Jesus, please save me!" And he came. At first there was a tiny little speck of light in the darkness, and it very rapidly got bright. The light became so bright that if it were in this world, it would have consumed me. It just would have fried me to a crisp. It wasn't at all hot or dangerous there. The light just came upon me… he was in this light, and he reached down out of this light, and gently started to pick me up. And in his light, I could see that I had sores and filth and wounds all over. I looked like roadkill. And he was gently putting his hands underneath me and very tenderly picking me up, and as he was touching me, everything just went away. All the wounds, all the pain, all the dirt—it just evaporated away. And I was whole and healed, and inside, filled with his love—which I wish I could be more articulate about. It is so frustrating not being able to tell people about it because it's the best thing that ever happened to me in my life. It's the everything, it's the all of life is to know that love, and I get to it, and I can't describe it. I can't convey it to you.

He was holding me and embracing me, rubbing my back, like a father would his son, like a mother would her daughter, just gently rubbing my back. And I was bawling like a baby, out of happiness—the release of having been lost, and now been found, having been dead, and now brought back to life. And then he carried me out of there. Up we went, out, gone. And we were moving towards a world of light, and I began to have thoughts of tremendous shame, that I had been *so* bad. I thought of myself as dirt, garbage, filth. And I thought to myself, he has made a mistake. I don't belong here. He doesn't want me. You know, like the shame of it, how could he care about me? Why me? I'm bad. And we stopped. We weren't in Hell. We weren't in Heaven. We were in between. And we stopped, and he said, "We don't make mistakes. You belong here."

And we began to converse, and he was talking with me and telling me things, and he brought over some angels. And we went over my life, from beginning to end. And what they wanted to show me in my life is what I had done right and what I had done wrong. And without going through my whole life story, it was real simple. When I had been a loving, kind person, considerate of other people, it made the angels happy, it made Jesus happy, and they let me know that it made God happy. And when I had been selfish and manipulative, it made the angels unhappy, it made Jesus unhappy, and they let me know that it made God unhappy. What they were trying to convey to me in a nutshell was, the whole purpose of my existence had been to love God and love my neighbor as myself. That's why I had been created. That's what I was in this world to do and to learn, and I had failed. They told me that I had to come back to this world. I got real upset because I wanted to go to Heaven. What they told me about Heaven was, it is the most fun, most interesting place, most wonderful place. Everybody would want to go to Heaven, and I wanted to get there. And they said that I wasn't ready, I wasn't fit, that it wasn't my time to go to Heaven. It was my time to come back to this world and try and live the way that God wanted me to live, the way that God had created me to live in the first place.

I told them (Jesus and the angels) that I could not live in this world without them. I said that my heart would break to send me back to this world, because they would be there, and I would be here. And they said to me, "You don't get it? What is the matter? We have been showing you all these things; we have explained it to you. We've always been there. We have always been with you, all this time. You have never been alone down there." I said, "You've got to let me know that you're around once in awhile." They said, if I prayed, and confessed my sins to God, and gave what I had… what they meant by what I had was, gave my worries, my cares, my hopes, my dreams, just gave it all up to God, that there would be times when they would be there, and I would know in my heart that they were there. I wouldn't necessarily see them again, but I would feel the love like I had felt it then. And I said that if you will assure me that there would be times when I can know that love, I could live in this world. And they said that they would do that. And with that, they sent me back.

After the experience, the nurse who had been in the room a few minutes before and said they couldn't find a doctor, she came running back in the room and said a doctor had arrived at the hospital… This was all pretty miraculous stuff. This is now around 9:30 at night. She said, "The doctor has arrived at the hospital, and we are going to do surgery on you right away." And some orderlies and people came in, and they threw my wife out of the room. It was very disturbing, because I was trying to tell them, and I wanted to tell my wife what had happened to me. When I passed my wife in the hall on the gurney on the way to surgery, I said, "Everything is going to be great!" And she just started bawling, because she thought it was like a dying man saying his last words.

The strange thing about the experience is the memory hasn't dulled at all. It's real intense. It stays intense. And I believe that one of the reasons that God gave me this experience is so that I would have an opportunity to share it with someone. I don't know who, I never know who. But I would have the opportunity to share it with somebody so that it could be of help to them.[7]

WHY DOES HELL EVEN EXIST?

The basic purpose of Hell is not a place of punishment, but a place designed to make you realize that choosing darkness, or a separation from your divine source, is not what you want. It is there to convince you to choose light. Or in simplest terms, Hell exists to be as scary as possible so that you choose Heaven. I use the terms "Hell" and "Heaven" quite often in this book, but in a manner of speaking, there is only "the other side of the veil." There, the collective consciousnesses of spiritual beings can create any environment they want. Based on the intentions they set, they create many different environments in the spiritual world. I refer collectively to the unpleasant environments as "Hell," and the desirable ones as "Heaven." But just two places, as in one or the other... It is not quite that simple.

There is one last item I need to mention about Hell. I have no direct evidence to support this theory, but I do have plenty of indirect evidence and one *very* strong feeling in the deepest part of my soul. I do not believe that Hell is a permanent sentence for anyone. It is only there to teach a soul that separation from love is undesirable in the worst way possible. It exists only as part of the free will learning experience. No loving Father here on Earth would sentence his child to eternal torture, no matter how badly that child behaved, and God is far more merciful than any earthly Father. I do not believe that any soul will stay in Hell forever, even though it may feel like an eternity to any soul who is there. Some day, when they are ready, everybody comes home.

CHAPTER 3

HEAVEN

"Everyone who sees Heaven, even for one second, wants to stay forever, no matter how nice their life might be here on Earth."[8]

> — *Marvin J. Besteman,*
> *pancreatic tumor*

ARRIVING IN HEAVEN

It is quite common for people to be greeted in Heaven by friends or relatives who passed on before them, or sometimes even by large groups of people that include distant relatives they had never met while on Earth.

The place that I was in had no ceiling. It was just blue sky up above. There were about 150 to 200 people there, and they were beautiful. They were SO thrilled to see me. Nobody has ever been that thrilled to see me. They were all applauding and many of them were crying. Every one of them had to hug me, some two or three times had to hug me. I hugged every one of them. They were communicating an affection, a level of affection that I've never had before, ever.

— Chris, heart attack

IMPOSSIBLE TO DESCRIBE

Heaven cannot be described in earthly terms. It would be far easier to explain a rainbow to a person who has been blind since birth or explain a symphony to a man who has been deaf since birth. No matter how hard you try, you can't explain it. Describing the real world from within the dream is an impossible task. That is how Heaven is. You must experience it to understand it. You could listen to thousands of near-death experiencers try to describe the other side of the veil, but it would not matter. When you get there, you will still be in for the shock of your life… And it's going to be a good one.

HOW TO GET THERE

Live your life with love. That's it. It's that simple. I know there are going to be a lot of religious people who don't like that answer, but the reason for this hypothesis will be discussed more in depth in the chapter on religion. For now, I will only mention that most religions can be used effectively as a tool to guide you on a path to Heaven, but it is definitely not the religion itself that gets you there.

Even after hearing more than 700 testimonies, it is not entirely clear to me why some people we might judge as evil, end up in Heaven. It definitely does not have anything to do with the particular religion a person chooses, but it does seem to have a lot to do with a person's heart. Ironically, if a person is worried about going to Hell, that's usually a good indication that they are going to Heaven! Worrying about going to Hell is a sign that a person is aware of the importance of being a good person and feels they may have failed. Those near-death experiencers who end up in Hell usually have no such thoughts of self-judgment or empathy towards other human beings.

I have heard several cases of people who were being drawn towards Hell, but then were physically pulled towards Heaven by an angelic being, or cried out for help, and were subsequently rescued.

If you are worried about going to Hell, let me set your mind at ease with the following examples of just some of the "bad" people who died and went to Heaven:

- A tyrannical atheist who openly cursed at others who believed in God

- A man who spent his entire life as a thief

- A man who murdered another in a fit of anger

- A woman who killed a mother of 3 young children

- A Nazi SS Officer who tortured and killed people in a concentration camp

Still worried about going to Hell? The kind of person that ends up in Hell would never even THINK of reading a book like this. You can relax. Paradise will be waiting for you when you leave this planet.

THE PEARLY GATES

Of the hundreds of testimonies I have heard, only a few people have mentioned the gates of Heaven. Because the spiritual realm is so different, they have difficulty describing it in earthly terms. They describe a very tall wall or barrier that appears to stretch in both directions to infinity. The gates themselves are made of something that looks similar to wood, only it has a shimmering and pearly appearance, and the material is somehow living or alive.

LEVELS

There are definitely various levels of Heaven, but it is not clear from the testimonies how many there are. The first level of Heaven is laid out somewhat like Earth. It has streets of transparent gold, houses, buildings, cathedrals, trees, mountains, flowers, rivers, lakes, waterfalls, parks, forests, animals, and everything else you could imagine. Each higher level of Heaven is more amazing and wondrous than the previous one, but even the first level of Heaven is so much different than Earth, that it is very difficult to describe in earthly words. As such, this book will only address the first level of Heaven in an attempt to give a basic description of what it is like and what activities take place there. But let's just for a moment address a far more important issue. Is there baseball in Heaven?

BASEBALL IN HEAVEN

Jim and Bob were the world's most fanatic baseball fans. They went to every local baseball game together, and each year they made a special trip to see the World Series in person. They were such fanatics that one day they made a pact with each other; whoever died first was to return to Earth as a ghost and tell the other one if there was in fact, baseball in Heaven. Years later, Jim died and returned a few days later as a ghost, waking up his friend Bob from a sound sleep. Bob, forgetting their pact and stunned to see his dead friend appearing as a ghostly figure at the side of his bed asked, "Jim, what are you doing here!?" Jim replied, "Bob, I have good news and bad news. The good news is, there is baseball in Heaven. The bad news is, you're pitching in this Friday's game."

So why is this joke amusing? For a person who has been in Heaven for all eternity and never lived an earthly life, the joke would make no sense at all. We on Earth mistakenly believe that Earth is the happening place to be, the preferred and the desired life, the best of the best there is. And, as nice a place as Heaven might be, it would be boring and uninteresting compared to Earth. After all, who wants to be dead? Who wants to live all eternity as a ghost with no real substance and no contact with the real world?

> "Love is a sign from the Heavens that you are here for a reason. If I lived a billion years more, in my body or yours, there is not a single experience on Earth that could ever be as good as being dead. Nothing."[9]
>
> *— Dr. Dianne Morrissey,*
> *after her near-death experience*

The conception Hollywood shows us of Heaven is absurd. We don't all float around in white gowns in the clouds playing harps all day long. Heaven is the most peaceful, beautiful, joyous, adventurous, fun, exciting, and wondrous place that anybody could possibly imagine. Everyone who has been there, even for just a moment, wants to stay there forever. And as far as being a ghost or spirit goes, the experience of Heaven is far more real and substantial than anything here on Earth. It is the absolute height of reality and considered the "real world" by all those who have visited it.

It certainly seems to me that many people who say they are going to Heaven don't seem to really believe it. If they did, why are they so afraid to die? When talking about people who have died, they say things like, "He is in a better place." If they really believe that Heaven is a better place, wouldn't they be anxious to get there and even envious of those who have died before them? Near-death experiencers are! Every single person who has seen Heaven has one thing in common—they realize the great importance of life on

Earth, but when they think about death, they are looking forward to it as something wonderful. They have no fear of death.

Years ago, my friend and her three children were involved in a car accident, and her 13-year-old daughter died. In his love, God gave my friend confirmation that her daughter went straight to Heaven. Yet still, she says that she "lost" her daughter. This is a misleading statement. When a person dies, we know exactly where they are, and we know we will see them again. So how is that lost? A more accurate statement would be to say that there is a temporary separation. That's all it really is.

But even knowing what a beautiful place Heaven is, it still hurts to be separated from a loved one. Today I did no writing other than this paragraph as I am personally feeling the pain of that separation. My mother left this world and entered Paradise this morning at 8 a.m., Monday, May 26, 2014. If I thought her existence had been extinguished, the emotional pain would be unbearable. But I know she is happier than she ever had been in her life on Earth. Some people say, "She's in a place of eternal rest." They couldn't be more wrong.

WORK IN HEAVEN?!

People in Heaven report being very busy with many tasks and activities. Yes, you will have a job in Heaven. For some people such as teachers, artists, or healers, there may be some similarities to your earthly work, but for most, it won't at all be like the job you have now. Here we have a very defined distinction between work and leisure. You have your job that you'd probably never do voluntarily if you were independently wealthy. Many of us don't like our jobs and drudge through the day looking forward to 5 o'clock, when we can have some time to ourselves. But in Heaven there is no distinction between work and play because the two are one in the same. Each person enthusiastically looks forward to the pleasure and joy of doing their job because it's exactly what they love to do, and they are good at doing it. Every individual in Heaven has a unique set of experiences and talents and works on tasks according to those talents and activities they enjoy doing. Although it may be difficult to believe, no one else in all of Heaven will be able to do your job as well as you can! But as "busy" as people are in Heaven, it is not at all stressful or unpleasant. A good analogy would be when you go to an amusement park or go on vacation somewhere, and you fill your agenda with all the things you want to see and do because you don't want to miss out on any of the fun. That's what doing your job in Heaven is like. It is far better than the best possible fantasy that you can imagine for yourself here on Earth.

THE SIZE

I recall one near-death experiencer describing the size of Heaven in terms I could understand. I wish I would have written down the dimensions, but I remember at the time doing a rough calculation in my head and determining that Heaven was at least 10,000 times the size of the Earth, with, of course, infinite room to expand. It doesn't occupy space in the physical dimension, so there is no restraint on growth because of a lack of real estate. And there are many other Heavenly realms, not just the one described in this book.

THE SENSES

People in Heaven have a clarity of thought unmatched by anything experienced during life on Earth. Logic and reasoning appear to be unnecessary in the spirit world because there you simply know that you know. There is no doubt. All you have to do is ponder something, and the answer comes to your mind as if it were something you always knew. People in Heaven meet distant relatives they never met on Earth and instantly recognize them knowing exactly who they are.

Vision is greatly enhanced. Not only can people see more clearly, but our spiritual eyes can look at a flower on a mountainside 50 miles away and count every petal. Blind spots disappear completely. Although a person might focus on a single object, he can see 360 degrees in all directions, including behind him.

BLIND SINCE BIRTH

> I felt like it was a nightmare because I have never been accustomed to perceiving of anything from a distance. I touch things and my world is at arm's length. I perceive of everything tactilely and I couldn't translate what it was that I was receiving, and it was scary. A lot of people have asked me, "Wasn't it wonderful to see?" Actually, no, it wasn't, it was terrible initially. There were trees, and there were birds, and there were quite a few people, but they were all made out of light. And I could see, and it was incredible—really beautiful. I was overwhelmed by that experience because I couldn't really imagine what light was like.
>
> *— Vickie, car accident*

Of the hundreds of near-death experiences that I have heard, two of them were from people who were blind since birth. During their experiences, they could see for the first time. They were not able to say which colors they saw because they have never learned what colors go with which name. They could only describe what they saw as different intensities and shades of light and color.

COLORS

> The closer I got, the more peace and love and joy I
> felt. I saw this huge, beautiful city. I felt love like I've
> never felt it before. I heard people talking and kids were
> playing. I heard a waterfall. I saw these colors I have
> never seen before in my life; beautiful, radiant colors.

— Tony, drive-by shooting

Many people who have visited Heaven remark about the amazing colors there. They say there are rich pastels and beautiful vibrant colors unlike anything we have here on Earth. They can't describe the colors to us, any more than we could describe what colors look like to a person who can only see in black and white.

It took me years of listening to testimonies to finally get an explanation of the sheer number of colors in Heaven. We have three primary colors: Yellow, Blue, and Red. Various mixtures of these three colors form all the colors we have here on Earth. One man who had a near-death experience noticed that there are over 80 primary colors in Heaven. Even when near-death experiencers mention colors in Heaven that we know of, they describe them as richer and more vibrant than those same colors on Earth. One man said he saw a field of grass that was the most dazzling color of green he had ever seen.

HEARING

Hearing becomes dramatically enhanced with the ability to hear tones and frequencies far beyond that of our earthly ears. People in Heaven can look down at Earth and actually listen to conversations from afar. But the sense of hearing is more useful for appreciating the beautiful music of Heaven. Communication in the spiritual realm is done non-verbally and without language, directly from mind to mind. It is fast, efficient, and flawless—no possibility of any misunderstanding. Many people who have spoken with God have described it as a non-linear simultaneous download of huge amounts of information. A single instant of information could take days or even years to explain in human language. With this type of communication, it is absolutely impossible to have a misunderstanding.

MUSIC

The music in Heaven is sublime. I have heard that our most beautiful music here on Earth, by comparison, sounds like a child banging on a pan with a stick. They even have concerts in Heaven where thousands of people gather in stadium-like buildings and listen to master musicians play their divine music. The best description of the music in Heaven comes from Pastor Don Piper's near-death experience after his fatal car crash. The following is a direct quote from his book *90 Minutes in Heaven.*

> My most vivid memory of Heaven is what I heard. I can only describe it as a holy swoosh of wings. But I'd have to magnify that thousands of times to explain the effect of the sound in Heaven. It was the most beautiful and pleasant sound I've ever heard, and it didn't stop. It was like a song that goes on forever. I felt awestruck, wanting only to listen. I didn't just hear music. It seemed as if I were a part of the music and it played in and through my body. I stood still, and yet I felt embraced by the sounds.

> As aware as I became of the joyous sounds and melodies that filled the air, I wasn't distracted. I felt as if the Heavenly concert permeated every part of my being, and at the same time I focused on everything else around me.

I never saw anything that produced the sound. I had the sense that whatever made the Heavenly music was just above me, but I didn't look up. I'm not sure why. Perhaps it was because I was so enamored with the people around me, or maybe it was because my senses were so engaged that I feasted on everything at the same time. I asked no questions and never wondered about anything. Everything was perfect. I sensed that I knew everything and had no questions to ask.

Myriad sounds so filled my mind and heart that it's difficult to explain them. The most amazing one, however, was the angels' wings. I didn't see them, but the sound was a beautiful, holy melody with a cadence that seemed never to stop. The swishing resounded as if it was a form of never-ending praise. As I listened, I simply knew what it was.

A second sound remains, even today, the single, most vivid memory I have of my entire Heavenly experience. I call it music, but it was different from anything I had ever heard or expect to hear on the Earth. The melodies of praise filled the atmosphere. The non-stop intensity and endless variety overwhelmed me.

The praise was unending, but the most remarkable thing to me was that hundreds of songs were being sung at the same time, all of them worshiping God. As I approached the large, magnificent gate, I heard them from every direction and realized that each voice praised God. I write voice, but it was more than that. Some sounded instrumental, but I wasn't sure, and I wasn't concerned. Praise was everywhere, and all of it was musical, yet comprised of melodies and tones I'd never experienced before.

"Hallelujah! Praise! Glory to God! Praise to the King!" Such words rang out in the midst of all the music. I don't know if angels were singing them or if they came from humans. I felt so awestruck and caught up in the Heavenly mood that I didn't look around me. My heart filled with the deepest joy I've ever experienced. I wasn't a participant in the worship, yet I felt as if my heart rang out with the same kind of joy and exuberance. If we played three CDs of praise at the same time, we'd have a cacophony of noise that would drive us crazy. This was totally different. Every sound blended, and each voice or instrument enhanced the others.

As strange as it may seem, I could clearly distinguish each song. It sounded as if each hymn of praise was meant for me to hear as I moved inside the gates. Many of the old hymns and choruses I had sung at various times in my life were part of the music, along with hundreds of songs I had never heard before. Hymns of praise, modern-sounding choruses, and ancient chants filled my ears and brought not only a deep peace but the greatest feeling of joy I've ever experienced…

The celestial tunes surpassed any I had ever heard. I couldn't calculate the number of songs, perhaps thousands, offered up simultaneously, and yet there was no chaos, because I had capacity to hear each one and discern the lyrics and melody. I marveled at the glorious music. Though not possessed of a great singing voice in life, I knew that if I sang, my voice would be in perfect pitch and would sound as melodious and harmonious as the thousands of other voices and instruments that filled my ears.

Even now, back on Earth, sometimes I still hear faint echoes of that music. When I'm especially tired and lie in bed with my eyes closed, occasionally I drift off to sleep with the sounds of Heaven filling my heart and mind. No matter how difficult a day I've had, peace immediately fills every part of my being. I still have flashbacks, although they're different from what we normally refer to as flashbacks. Mine are more flashbacks of the sounds than the sights.

As I've pondered the meaning of the memory of the music, it seems curious. I would have expected the most memorable experience to be something I had seen or the physical embrace of a loved one. Yet above everything else, I cherish those sounds, and at times I think, I can't wait to hear them again in person. It's what I look forward to. I want to see everybody, but I know I'll be with them forever. I want to experience everything Heaven offers, but most of all, I want to hear those never-ending songs again.

In those minutes, and they held no sense of time for me, others touched me, and their warm embraces were absolutely real. I saw colors I would never have believed existed. I've never, ever felt more alive than I did then. I was home; I was where I belonged. I wanted to be there more than I had ever wanted to be anywhere on Earth. Time had slipped away, and I was simply present in Heaven. All worries, anxieties, and concerns vanished. I had no needs, and I felt perfect.[10]

ETERNITY

There is no time in Heaven. It is something that many near-death experiencers have tried to explain to me, but I've never fully understood it. They say that in this world we have what happened yesterday, what is happening right now, and what's going to happen tomorrow. But on the other side of the veil, it's all the same. There is no yesterday or tomorrow because everything is always happening in the present moment. It always has and it always will. Some describe it as instantly being aware of eternity, and others describe it as the "eternal now." They say it is an amazing experience, and that the absence of time feels wonderfully liberating.

The lack of time creates a few interesting scenarios that are impossible here on Earth. For instance, when people get together for whatever reason, nobody shows up early and nobody shows up late. That's because you can decide what "time" (for lack of a better word) you want to be there, and instantly you're there at that exact moment.

Because there is no time, there is no delay between thought and action. One man who was in Heaven had a thought about picking some flowers, but in the exact same instant he had the thought, he had already bent over, picked the flowers, and was holding them in his hand. Instead of action following thought, the two occur simultaneously.

NO MISTAKES

"I felt a harmony. There is a peace, harmony and well-being. Everything is in perfect flow."

— *Sharon, death under anesthesia.*

In Heaven, people don't make mistakes. Here on Earth, you are always keeping your guard up, always trying to do your best and avoid mistakes. But people make mistakes anyway, and there is always the temptation to misbehave. But this is not the case in Heaven. You can't make a mistake there because imperfection does not exist in that realm. You don't ever have to worry about doing the wrong thing or fouling things up. In every action and decision, you are constantly infused with the knowledge and wisdom such that mistakes will never occur. In Heaven there is no sin, and there is no temptation to sin. Each person can let their guard down and relax completely in the knowledge that they will continue to exist, grow, and learn in complete perfection and harmony with others—infallible and perfect.

PARKS AND GARDENS

The parks and gardens in Heaven are exquisite and breathtakingly beautiful. One near-death experiencer described a park in Heaven as being very beautiful. When he was asked, "How beautiful? Like Yosemite National Park?" After thinking for a moment, he responded, "Maybe a hundred times more beautiful than Yosemite." Many describe beautiful varieties of colored flowers. Some flowers actually sing and all plants in Heaven have a consciousness, so you can converse with them if you'd like. My own aunt, who died and was revived while giving birth to my cousin, had a near-death experience. When she walked by what looked like a common house plant, the plant greeted her with an enthusiastic, "Hi!" She was shocked and said to the plant, "You can talk!" The plant responded, "Of course I can!"

People have described rivers of living water and great trees that tower into the sky far taller than our redwoods and giant sequoias. One woman who was walking through Heaven with her brother came to the edge of a river and asked how they were going to cross it. They had the option to float over it, but instead decided to walk right through it. She was not only surprised that she did not need air while underwater, but when she emerged from the river, her clothes were completely dry.

There are huge lakes, beautiful waterfalls, and majestic snow-capped mountains. Traveling from one place to another in Heaven is as easy as thinking about being in a place, and you are instantly transported there. Of course, you always have the option of walking, floating, or flying, and having all eternity, you are never in a hurry, so you can choose to travel as you wish.

PLEASE LITTER

There are no dead plants, brown leaves, trash, or litter of any kind in Heaven because the entire place is self-cleaning. One woman who was walking through Heaven picked a fruit off a tree and ate it. She described it is being similar to a peach, but much tastier. When she finished eating it, she threw the seed on the ground. As she did, she witnessed the seed instantly dissolve and disappear into the green grass. Heaven is always clean and beautiful. No yard work or cleaning required.

LIGHT IN HEAVEN

There is no sun or moon in Heaven, but every object, plant, animal, human being, and spirit glows with its own light. Some beings glow so brightly that their auras shine through the walls and ceilings of their dwellings and can be seen from the outside.

There are magnificent buildings made of translucent-colored jewels all glowing from within. People who have seen the cathedrals in Heaven often remark how they copy the ones here on Earth. But it is exactly the opposite—we copy them. At some subconscious level, human beings are aware of what Heavenly cathedrals look like, so we try to make ours look similar. Since we don't have any translucent colored crystals that glow with their own light, we use the closest thing we have on Earth—stained glass.

BACK TO SCHOOL

There is something resembling schools in Heaven, complete with instructors, lessons, and a display similar to our chalkboards and multimedia displays. Just as there are laws of physics, there are also laws of consciousness. One of the first concepts they teach newcomers in Heaven is that *thoughts are things.* You will be taught using the power of your mind how to think physical objects into existence by nothing other than the power of your own consciousness. For instance, if you want to create an apple, you close your eyes and imagine a form of white light and energy in your hand and then slowly imagine that white ball of light and energy forming itself into an apple. As you do this, the apple will actually form in your hand. Using this method, you will be able to change your house and do any redecorating or remodeling that you would like, using the power of your mind. Entire houses and buildings in Heaven are constructed using pure thought without any physical labor.

SEX

I have never heard a single testimony mention the actual act of sexual intercourse occurring in Heaven, but there is a kind of spiritual copulation or joining of souls that some people have described. It is far more intimate and pleasurable than sexual intercourse here on Earth. Basically, you can merge with any spirit, angelic being, human being, animal, or plant, and you can experience each other completely. If you merge with another person for example, you will receive and experience the essence of who that person is including all their thoughts, feelings, talents, and the things they enjoy. The experience is so emotionally and spiritually intimate that upon merging with another person you immediately "fall in love" with the unique expression of creation that they represent.

One young girl who merged with a rose in Heaven recounted how she experienced the life of that rose, how overjoyed the rose was to be part of creation, the pleasure the rose felt in participating in the beautification of Heaven and providing something pleasing for others to look at. She experienced, firsthand, exactly what it is like to be a rose in Heaven. For those of you who have a relative that you did not get along with on Earth, even if you stopped speaking to each other, in Heaven you will understand each other completely and have nothing but compassion for each other. The reconciliation will not be a traumatic one, but more light-hearted and humorous. Each one will perfectly understand each other's point of view and the reasons why they did the things they did. With such understanding comes instantaneous forgiveness and acceptance. The two of you will probably be laughing with each other at the trivialities that caused the falling out in the first place.

FOREVER YOUNG

In the first level of Heaven where you still have a body, your Heavenly body will be nothing like your body here on Earth. Regardless of how old a person is when they die, they are young, healthy, and energetic in Heaven. I recall one woman who said she saw her grandmother during her visit to Heaven. On Earth, her grandmother was elderly with wrinkled skin, gray hair, hunched over, and no teeth. She recognized her grandmother in Heaven, but she looked nothing like the elderly woman she remembered. The woman she saw was young, mid-20s, with long black hair, and when she smiled, she had a full set of white teeth. Her grandmother was young and stunningly beautiful.

Absolute perfect health is a wonderful side benefit of being in Heaven. Most near-death experiencers say that the people they met in Heaven all appeared to be in their mid twenties or younger. There are children in Heaven as well as older spirits and angels.

One seven-year-old girl who had died from an infection and high fever, was being taken to Heaven through the tunnel by her brother who had died in the Vietnam War. She noticed that there were other people with them in the tunnel. Some were calmly excited as she was, but others were so ecstatic that they were dancing for joy. The little girl asked her brother, "Why are they so happy?" Her brother explained to her that those were elderly people who were in bodies that were very old, restrictive, broken down, and full of pain. And now they are overjoyed to be pain-free, young, and healthy again.

THE PEOPLE YOU WILL MEET

> "And then, a greeting: 'Hello, Marv. Welcome to Heaven. My name is Peter.' Standing before me was one of my best-loved scriptural figures, the hot-headed Apostle Peter... who I must say was a little bit shaggy looking."[11]

Nobody really seems to be too surprised about meeting dead relatives in Heaven, but a few are shocked when they arrive and are greeted by not only friends and relatives, but also pets they had while on Earth. Even more shocking is that they can have conversations with those former pets. Not only do pets go to Heaven, but people regularly interact with other animals in Heaven that would normally be dangerous on Earth. One near-death experiencer saw some children playing in a park with a big lion as if it were a domesticated cat.

Other people meet distant relatives in Heaven they never knew on Earth, such as great-great-grandparents. They are told stories about how their ancestors crossed over from Europe to the United States. Some heard the tales of their ancestors who were instrumental in pioneering the country when it was young.

CHILDREN YOU NEVER HAD

It is quite common for women to meet children they never knew they had, who were the result of miscarriages or abortions. As one woman arrived in Heaven, she was greeted by a young girl who said, "Hi, Mommy!" The woman apologized to the little girl explaining, "I'm so sorry, honey. I'm not your mother. I don't have any children." The little girl responded, "Yes, you do! I'm the child you aborted." The woman began to cry because she had an abortion when she was very young, and for many years had felt guilty about killing her own unborn child. But her daughter responded, "It's okay Mommy. I forgave you. And besides, I really like it up here."

Of course, the one person many people speak about meeting in Heaven is Jesus himself. Apparently, since there is no time in Heaven, Jesus can spend one-on-one personal time with individuals, and often does. However, Jesus is not like the religions portray him. He stands as an example of a "master soul" and encourages others to follow in his footsteps. One near-death experiencer saw Jesus visit a classroom of students in Heaven. After Jesus left the classroom, the instructor told the students that one day, each and every one of them would all reach Jesus' level of spiritual development and purity. Many of the students were shaking their heads in awe and disbelief.

NO ANGRY GOD

For a long time, I was very angry at Christianity because I was taught about a God who was mostly like a strict disciplinarian father—loving, but very rigid with rules and regulations, and dishing out severe punishment for anyone making a mistake or defiling his authority in the slightest way. But God is the exact opposite. He is very loving, lighthearted, and easygoing—more like a loving and gentle Father who is caring and kind to his children, and very understanding when one of his children makes a mistake. People who have met Jesus say it is like talking to your best friend, and you can say absolutely anything to him. You feel completely comfortable and open and as relaxed as you can be. Many have said that he is very funny and has a wonderful sense of humor.

One man who was having a conversation with Jesus in Heaven accidentally used the word "shit." Immediately realizing his error, he asked Jesus, "Am I in trouble now?" Jesus' reaction was surprising. He laughed and said, "It's only a word, Son." But it is important to note here, the distinction between profanity and taking God's name in vain. When people are going through their life reviews and they use profanity, it might be viewed as undesirable or vulgar, but profanity is mostly just empty words. But when they get to parts of their life review when they curse using the name of God or Jesus, it makes the Heavenly spirits watching the review very grieved. Think about the person you love most on Earth—someone who has been the most kind, loving, gentle, and caring towards you in this life, maybe your mother or your best friend. Now imagine how you would feel if everyone else on Earth used that person's name as profanity. It would just hurt to hear such things.

APPRENTICESHIPS

In Heaven, one of the many activities you may participate in will be studying with a saint or master craftsman. You might learn about art, music, spiritual science, or heavenly engineering. You might even study to be one of those assigned to help people on Earth.

One man who visited Heaven was talking with his grandfather and asking him what they do in Heaven. His grandfather told him one of the things they really enjoy doing is helping people on Earth. In their spiritual bodies, the man and his grandfather came down to Earth where the man witnessed his father sitting in a meeting. The grandfather leaned over and said to his son, "You've got to get to that charity event." The man saw his father suddenly stop the meeting and announce that he was sorry but had to leave to catch a plane for a charity event he was speaking at.

PLAY TIME

It is not all work and no play in Heaven. There are games and leisure activities in Heaven, and even entire uninhabited planets where people go to play and frolic. There is a game in Heaven similar to *Red Rover*, where groups of people stand opposite each other and then run towards each other mixing and literally running through each other, experiencing the personalities and lives of each person they momentarily come in contact with. There are also places to go where people can rest and sleep, during which time their spirit and energy rejuvenates.

Although I have not spent a great deal of time talking about leisure and play in Heaven, the spirit world is one of humor and fun. Even the business and work that is done there is nothing like the stressful business environments here on Earth. There, work is done, and business is conducted in a lighthearted and easygoing way.

In a nutshell, Heaven is the most peaceful, beautiful, fun, exciting, adventurous, and wondrous place that anybody could possibly imagine. When given the option to return to Earth, it is very difficult for anyone to leave.

OTHER REALMS

It is important to note that just as our consciousness creates the dreams we experience when we sleep, and mankind's collective consciousness creates the earthly environment we now live in, the collective consciousness of all those in the spiritual world also creates the environments of Heaven and Hell. Technically speaking, there really is no Heaven or Hell. There are only spiritual realms that are created by the collective consciousness of those residing in those realms. Our human thinking is very linear and three dimensional, thus we tend to label things and put them in a box. We refer to the higher vibrational realms that are positive as "Heaven" and lower vibrational realms that are unpleasant as "Hell." But in reality, there are no limits to the imagination and creativity of those in the spiritual world. There are many other mysterious and fascinating realms that number greater than the stars in the heavens and cannot be described in earthly words. Few near-death experiencers have ever been shown these other realms, but they do exist—and more are continually being created by the consciousnesses of those who choose to explore the limitlessness of their creativity and imagination.

CHAPTER 4

BACK TO EARTH

"After I came back, my whole world was blown to pieces. Everything I thought I knew about myself, about life, about the afterlife, about religion—it was all gone."

— Nanci, breast cancer

THERE IS NO WAY I'M GOING BACK

That's usually the response when a person is given a choice to either stay in Heaven or go back to Earth. But I am grateful that so many people came back. Had it not been for those who returned, I would have never learned the spiritual lessons described in this book and my life would not be filled with the tremendous love and peace that I now experience.

For those who are told they have to go back, they often argue and protest trying every reason imaginable for why they should stay in Heaven. Even a woman with a newborn baby will often protest being sent back to Earth. Some people are told that they have unfinished work on Earth. Others are told that they are not ready, or it is not their time to go to Heaven.

On the other hand, some people are told that they have finished their work and can choose to remain in Heaven. But our spiritual guides in Heaven are quite wise and experienced when dealing with humans, and they know exactly how we think. They will often show a person what their purpose is on Earth and the benefits that humanity will receive if they return. At this point, many decide they *must* return to Earth to continue their work. Interestingly enough, the memories of that purpose and mission are usually taken away from the person when they return. They remember being shown their purpose, but they cannot remember what that purpose was. Apparently, we are not supposed to know exactly what our jobs on Earth are, but those who choose to return are assured that they will receive all the guidance from Heaven needed to accomplish their purpose.

BACK TO THE BODY

Returning to Earth is an exceedingly unpleasant experience. During the return trip, people describe a feeling of losing much of the Heavenly knowledge and wisdom they had received while there. For those who are in great physical pain or who were involved in accidents, coming back to Earth involves returning to all the pain and anguish of their ailing bodies. The contrast between Heavenly bliss and an ailing physical body is intolerable. Even those whose bodies who are not in pain describe the return to a physical body as being very restrictive and uncomfortable, and they especially dislike the heavy feeling of gravity. Some people describe entering their body with a thud, and most people describe the return trip as happening very quickly or much faster than the trip *to* Heaven.

One woman who had a near-death experience during surgery to remove a brain aneurysm was so disgusted by her lifeless body that she refused to return to it. Her uncle, who had been her guide in Heaven, pushed her back into her body. There have been several cases where a heart attack patient upon being revived scolded the doctor for reviving them, saying things like, "You ruined everything! I was in absolute bliss. You had no right to bring me back."

ON FIRE WITH LOVE

One element that makes the return trip easier is the feeling people bring back with them from Heaven.

> When I came back, my heart was filled, and I would describe it as being on fire—my heart felt like it was on fire with love. The sensation of love that I experienced during my out of body experience has retained itself. I'm there. It is in me. It hasn't gone away. It hasn't changed.[12]

> *— Gordon, congestive heart failure*

Often at the scene of an accident when a person has returned from their near-death experience, although they are experiencing pain, their heart is filled with love for everyone and everything. They have a great peace and knowing that everything will be fine—that they are protected and immortal. They are sometimes perplexed or dismayed at why the people around them are so stressed and worried about their injuries.

TALKING ABOUT THE EXPERIENCE

Some people try to tell others what just happened to them, only to be met with responses like, "Just relax, you've been through a traumatic experience" or "No, you were just hallucinating." They very quickly learn that most people are highly skeptical, and will not believe their stories, and so they learn to keep silent about their heavenly experience.

Others are unable to talk about the experience because it is too emotionally difficult. Whenever they try to talk about it, they break down crying unable to get the words out. Even if a near-death experiencer finds a person who will listen and believe them, they have great difficulty in describing their heavenly experience in earthly words and tend to get very frustrated as a result. Some don't even try, saying that the experience is too ineffable, and that any description would fall far short of accurately conveying what they experienced.

DIFFICULTY ADJUSTING

The time after my near-death experience was probably the most frustrating six months of my existence. After experiencing perfection and something so beautiful, I wanted to hold on to it. I didn't want to let it go, and it wasn't easy. Everything seemed to change. It was almost like if I was starting my whole life over again. My first frustrating experience was with the television. I couldn't watch television. There would be a cosmetic commercial and I'd have to turn it off because it was something false. It was unnecessary. It just didn't belong and was insignificant. Any type of violence, like an old western movie, I would have to turn it off, because to me, that was total ignorance. There was just no reason on Earth to show people killing people.

— Joe, internal hemorrhaging after surgery

Joe's experience is not unusual. Many people long to go back to Heaven and become very depressed living on Earth. The depression can become severe and usually lasts for a few months to several years. In an attempt to return to Heaven, a few have tried committing suicide—only to be strictly warned by God that they are not to decide when they will die—and then are sent back to Earth. For some, especially those who have extended near-death experiences or multiple experiences, the readjustment process can be even more difficult. It can take years for them to recover and feel normal again.

> When I came back, I could not relate to this world. It took me the longest time. It was almost as if I was still over there. I couldn't recognize my children. I had no concept of eating. Everything was completely foreign. Truly in my case, I was lost between worlds. And the only logical thought that got through to me, believe it or not, was money. Three days later, it hit me with thunder that I had to go to work. My job was my only source of income, and I had to get up out of my bed and go to work.
>
> — *Phyllis, excessive bleeding*
> *from a miscarriage*

LOVE FOR ALL

Children learn at a young age the concept of limited resources. If there are three cookies and four children, they know that someone will be left without a cookie. Our culture tends to apply the same concept when it comes to love and relationships. Intimate loving relationships on Earth are assumed to be exclusive. Most people have the idea that their best friend couldn't possibly love them with all their heart if that friend also loves 10 other people just as much. But many near-death experiencers come back from Heaven with their hearts full of overflowing, unconditional love for all people. This tends to make their closest friends, family members, and spouses feel jealous and less important by comparison. We have phrases like "family first" and "my best friend." But for near-death experiencers there is a dissolution of boundaries because they are cognitively aware that the ideas of individuality and separateness are only illusions. They know that everybody on Earth is a family member, one human race, interconnected and all living on the same planet. They tend to treat everybody equally with an abundance of love. They often lose many friends and make new ones, and this becomes a process of turmoil and difficulty for their loved ones.

TRUSTING EVERYONE

It is very, very hard to put into words. I literally felt that I was shown everything in the world, everything in the universe, and how it fits together and how we continue. And when I came back, I felt that I loved everybody around me. I loved the trees. I felt a part of it. But I was very overwhelmed by the hate, and the anger, and the pain that is in this world. Everywhere I turned I wanted companionship and brotherhood, and everywhere I turned there were walls. I wanted to reach out and hug people and be with them, but nobody wanted this or understood it. I just felt like I was connected to humanity, but humanity wasn't connected to me.

— Glenn, crushed by a military transport

It becomes difficult for some near-death experiencers to relate to others. Because they feel a great connection to their fellow man, they want to reach out and show love to everyone they meet. But you can't go around hugging strangers and being unusually kind with people you don't know because it raises suspicion and leaves you vulnerable. We live in a world full of people, businesses, and governments, some of whom are out to manipulate and abuse others for their own malevolent purposes. During their adjustment periods, many near-death experiencers are overly trusting of their fellow man, and some get taken advantage of by others.

LIFE CHANGES

When they do return, the story becomes very interesting from the point of view of human psychology, because we find that these patients are profoundly changed. They are endowed with a totally new value structure. Whatever was in their lives before that they had been chasing, whether it was money or power or fame or any of these other things that people seek, they say that after this experience, their value is to primarily love others and seek loving relationships with their fellow human beings. And also they tell us that they have no more fear of death whatsoever.[13]

CAREER AND MARRIAGE CHANGES

Many near-death experiencers get divorced after their experience, because they become completely different people and are now incompatible with their spouses. If the marriage does survive, it continues in a much different way. Near-death experiencers tend to change their careers as well, favoring more altruistic pursuits. One police officer became a high school teacher. A billionaire financier gave up all ties with the business community to become a qualified counselor. A man involved in organized crime became a counselor for delinquent youths. An art teacher and former atheist became a pastor in the United Church of Christ.

A NEAR PERFECT MEMORY

As I've gotten older my memory just isn't what it used to be—so much so that I can actually hide my own Easter eggs. For near-death experiencers, their memory of the events stays very clear. They can recount the finest details of the experience even 20 years later. The spiritual realm is far more real than the physical world, which probably accounts for their vivid and long-lasting memories of the event.

SUPERPOWERS

The most unusual after effect near-death experiences return with is special abilities. Some can accurately sense the feelings and emotions of other people, and some can see auras or spiritual entities here on Earth. One man, as he walked into a church, saw hundreds of angels near the ceiling glowing brightly as the congregation sang praise music. Those who return from Heaven tend to have a higher sense of intuition, and sometimes gain insights into the future. Several times near-death experiencers have accurately predicted future events. A few have the ability to communicate with spirits or dead relatives from the other side. Others seem to have both physical and psychological healing abilities and make careers out of being spiritual counselors and healers.

Shortly after he had his near-death experience, a very good friend of mine was in a grocery store one day and saw a woman there. He got a vision of a gold ring in a dark and dusty place. He could see what looked like a grid or a grating, with light coming through, and suspected that the location of this ring was underneath a refrigerator. Somewhat hesitant and apprehensive, he approached the woman and told her of his vision. Without saying a word, the woman took out her cell phone and called her daughter at home asking her to look under the refrigerator. A few moments later as she hung up the phone and began to cry for joy, she explained to my friend, "My mother died recently, and I have been very upset with myself for losing her wedding ring. I don't know who you are or how you knew that but thank you!"

MY FAVORITE KIND OF PEOPLE

Near-death experiencers are absolutely my favorite kind of people to be around. They are not perfect; they still get depressed, frustrated, angry, jealous, selfish, or act out of fear. But those negative qualities that we all have seem to be far less prevalent in those who have visited Heaven. For the most part, I have found near-death experiencers to be spiritual people. They are non-judgmental, kind, loving, generous, altruistic, compassionate, and generally wonderful people to be around. But the good news is that you don't have to have a near-death experience to acquire all those good qualities. People who study near-death experiences, or those who are simply on a spiritual journey actively seeking God and making an effort to live in harmony with their environment and their fellow man, tend to take on these same positive qualities. And whether it is a near-death experiencer or someone like you on a spiritual journey, each person who becomes spiritually enlightened elevates all of humanity. I am grateful and thankful for all those on Earth who are fostering love.

CHAPTER 5

RELIGION

"The religion of the future will be a cosmic religion. It should transcend personal God and avoid dogma and theology."

— *Albert Einstein*

Anyone who investigates near-death experiences will eventually discover spiritual revelations that are not in line with whatever religion they subscribe to. The realities of God and Heaven are absolutely beautiful, but they are very different from what most religions teach. One reason science and religion have advanced so slowly is that they are not willing to open their minds enough to contemplate far from what they believe.

Trying to match the spiritual lessons from near-death experiencers' testimonies to the Bible or any specific religion is a dauntingly impossible task. Many religions accurately encompass basic spiritual truths, but much like this book, they don't have all the answers. If you are a member of one of the Judeo-Christian religions of the world, let me put your mind at ease with one statement: Everything I have learned from near-death experiencers reinforces the single overwhelmingly important idea that Jesus so concisely described when he was asked what the greatest commandment is—love God, and love your neighbor as yourself.

RELIGIOUS WAR

Many of the religions of this world are a wonderful benefit to humanity. They help people get closer to God, promote spiritual development, and are charitable to the needy and impoverished. But there are several major issues with religions that cause some serious problems.

"We are all one human race. There is no room for hatred."

— Wayne Irvine

One big problem are those radical elements of some religions that are under the mistaken impression that it is their sacred duty to kill in the name of God. Throughout history there have been various crusades, holy wars, and leaders committing horrible atrocities in the name of God. Even Adolf Hitler once said, "I believe today that my conduct is in accordance with the will of the Almighty Creator." But there is nothing at all "holy" about war. During many near-death experiencers' visits to Heaven, God made it very clear that he detests war and wants us to find peaceful ways to work out our differences. He even mentioned to a few people that many more wars would have occurred had it not been for heavenly intervention. Sometimes wisdom can come from the strangest places. The following is an excerpt from *The Onion News*, an Internet news company that exclusively does spoof news stories for the purposes of entertainment.

GOD ANGRILY CLARIFIES "DON'T KILL" RULE
SEP 26, 2001

"I don't care how holy somebody claims to be," God

said. "If a person tells you it's My will that they kill someone, they're wrong. Got it? I don't care what religion you are, or who you think your enemy is, here it is one more time: No killing, in My name or anyone else's, ever again. I tried to put it in the simplest possible terms for you people, so you'd get it straight, because I thought it was pretty important," said God, called Yahweh and Allah respectively in the Judaic and Muslim traditions. "I guess I figured I'd left no real room for confusion after putting it in a four-word sentence with one-syllable words, on the tablets I gave to Moses. How much more clear can I get? There are a ton of different religious traditions out there, and different cultures worship Me in different ways. But the basic message is always the same: Christianity, Islam, Judaism, Buddhism, Shintoism... every religious belief system under the sun, they all say you're supposed to love your neighbors, folks! It's not that hard a concept to grasp."[14]

Although meant to be a joke, the news story makes a valid point. God does not want us committing acts of violence in his name. I will go one step further; not only is killing others completely against God's will, even if you are involved in nothing more than a heated debate about religion, you have completely missed the entire focus of what religion is meant to be. Any time you catch yourself blaming, justifying your actions, making someone else wrong, or defending your beliefs, you are on the wrong side of the equation. Upsetting somebody about their religious beliefs, however wildly inaccurate those beliefs may be from your perspective, is not an act of love. True love does not challenge or question another person's beliefs, but helps others facilitate enjoying and exploring their own perspective of God.

All of humanity is connected in a very special and intimate way. The idea that we are separate individuals is only an illusion of separateness for the purposes of learning certain lessons and enjoying unique experiences here on Earth. We are all made from the same substance and come from the same source of all that is. Any philosophy or religious doctrine that separates us is generally not from God. Each religion should recognize they are only a tool to get closer to God, and there is nothing wrong with choosing a different tool to accomplish the same task. Every culture and every person is different, so they choose different religions and methods to learn about God.

RELIGION IS A TOOL

Most major religions mistakenly believe that their religion is the only correct one and the only way to salvation. They tend to view all other religions as misguided or blasphemous. Nothing could be further from the truth. This is not to say that religions contain no truth in them. On the contrary, religions contain a great deal of truth and spiritual insight. No person or organization can understand and know God completely. Just as the spiritual insights provided in this book are guesswork at best, so is anything about God that any religion teaches you. It is all speculation! God's gift of love is not exclusive to any religion, race, or doctrine.

While in Heaven, some near-death experiencers have asked which religion is the correct one, expecting to hear a particular faith such as Catholicism, Judaism, or Buddhism. But Heaven's answer to that question is always the same. The best religion for you is the one that brings you closest to God. If you are in a religion that is focused on love, you are on the right track. It is love within religion, not the religion itself, that creates spiritual growth.

CAPTAIN COOK'S BREW

In the 1700's, when European ships embarked on long voyages lasting several years, it was quite common for the ships to lose more than two thirds of their crew to scurvy—a disease resulting from a long-term lack of vitamin C. At the time no one was quite sure what caused scurvy, but they did know that a return to a normal diet on shore would cure it. In 1771 Captain Cook completed a four-year voyage successfully circumnavigating the globe without a single crewmember dying from scurvy, thanks to a special brew that he served to his crew on a regular basis. Captain Cook's brew contained an odd mixture of ingredients including malt, soap, vinegar, mustard, wheat, sauerkraut, and lemon syrup. The concoction worked, but mainly because of one ingredient. Lemon syrup is loaded with vitamin C. The rest of the ingredients had little or no effect.

Modern religions are not much different. They have a wide mixture of doctrines, rules, and regulations, which if followed, are supposed to effectively save your soul, and help you become a godly person. But there is really only one ingredient that makes the difference—love. In its many expressions and forms, love is what brings a person closer to God and grows a person's soul. Focusing on loving God and loving your neighbor is the key.

I find it odd that so many religions fail to recognize the validity of other religions, even when there is strong evidence in their own sacred books:

> "Beloved, let us love one another, for love is of God; and **everyone who loves is born of God and knows God**. He who does not love does not know God, for God is love."

> — *The Bible, 1 John 4: 7-8*

"Whoever destroys a soul, it is considered as if he destroyed the entire world. And **whoever saves a life**, it is considered as if he saved the entire world."

— Jewish Talmud,
Mishnah Sanhedrin 4:9; Tractate 37a

"Surely those who believe, and those who are Jews, and the Christians, and the Sabians, **whoever believes in God** and the Last day and does good, they shall have their reward from their Lord, and there is no fear for them, nor shall they grieve."

— Koran 2:62

Most of the world's major religions may have been inspired by God, and over time, were corrupted to some degree by man. This is why some religions tend to separate people, whereas love tends to unite people. Instead of trying to promote your particular religion, promote love to everyone you interact with. If you try to spread your religion to everyone you meet, you may have some limited success, but you will also encounter a great deal of resistance. But if you try to spread love to everyone you meet, their reaction will be overwhelmingly positive and accepting.

YOUR OWN PERSONAL GUIDE

God places in the heart of each and every person the knowledge of what is good and evil, or said a different way, love and fear. He does this through feelings. When a person is cruel, selfish, or manipulative with their fellow human beings, they feel at some soul-level the pain they are causing. We have evidence of this any time a person tries to conceal their behavior—they feel ashamed. But when a person treats others with love, kindness, peace, and patience, they feel good in their heart. This is God's built-in signal for us to follow the path of love. Through these signals, he gives each and every person on Earth a chance to accept him and follow him, or in other words, accept love and follow love, regardless of that person's religious or spiritual beliefs. He also has an army of angelic beings greater than the population of people on Earth, who are constantly speaking to us and guiding us. The angels encourage us to be kind, gentle, loving, forgiving, and exercise self-control. Every person is given an opportunity to choose love. Nobody goes to Hell without multiple chances to turn to God, even if they never recognize God as the love they are embracing. This may be how an atheist can go to Heaven. Any person, whether they believe in the entity of an all-powerful Creator or not, can be aware of our Creator in the form of love in their heart and can follow that love.

THE TRUE NATURE OF SIN

Some organized religions have doctrines consisting of a strict set of rules, and their members are taught that breaking any of these rules is a sin. Correspondingly, as long as you follow their rules, you are sin-free. The problem is, every religion has a different set of rules, and they can't all be correct.

Sin is basically any decision you make that is not in your best interest for promoting and advancing love in both yourself and others. In reality, everyone in Heaven expects us to sin a great deal. Neither God nor anyone in Heaven is angry with us for our dark moments. Even on our best days, the somewhat hostile atmosphere of this planet, along with our feeble human condition, make it nearly impossible to love everyone unconditionally all the time. Just as a parent who knows long before his child is born that his child will make many errors in life, God is well aware that we will make many mistakes. And just like any loving father, our father wants the best for us and would like us to avoid sin for our own well-being. And when we do sin, he wants us to learn from our mistakes, and hopefully avoid repeating them. So that's all sin is. It is just a path that isn't the best way to our own spiritual development and happiness. All of Heaven works diligently to help us and understands that sin and mistakes are part of the growing experience during this earthly existence. There is no need to get upset with yourself or others about making mistakes or sinning, because all of Heaven has an incredible amount of patience with us, just as we should have for ourselves and the people around us. The spiritual maturation process is long and arduous and cannot be rushed. So, relax and be patient with yourself and with others. When you see another person behaving in a way that you perceive to be unloving or inappropriate, recognize that they are on the same spiritual path we all walk on, moving towards the same ultimate goal. From your perspective, they may seem to be lagging very far behind you on that path, but you once stepped on the same ground they now walk on. You don't learn to live in enlightenment and love until you have passed through many experiences of darkness.

Of what use is any newborn child? They cannot talk, work, or contribute to society in any meaningful way. However, as they grow and mature, they can make great contributions to humanity, and those who are children now will someday rule this planet. But maturing takes time, patience, and the wisdom that comes from a lifetime of making many mistakes and errors along the way. Cut yourself and others **lots** of slack. After all, most of us are still just children, spiritually speaking.

HOMOSEXUALITY

Every major culture seems to be obsessed with human sexuality. Nobody looks at a dog walking down the street and says, "Oh my gosh.... it's a naked dog! The shame! The embarrassment! It's disgusting. Somebody call the police now!" But that's exactly what they would say and do if a naked man were walking down the street. They would probably go one step further and lock him up as if he were guilty of some heinous crime. So why is nudity so offensive? Very young children aren't embarrassed of nudity. Our culture teaches us to be ashamed of our own bodies.

As a result of our cultural obsession with sexuality, many religions and cultures have deemed homosexuality to be deviant or criminal behavior. In 78 countries, mostly located in Africa, Asia, and the Middle East, homosexuality is a punishable crime ranging from civil fines to the death penalty. For a long time, it was a punishable crime in most of the United States, although most of those laws have been repealed or declared unconstitutional.

Having been a born-again Christian for most of my life, I was taught that homosexuality was a sin and that gay people would go to Hell. It was a great surprise to me the first time I heard a near-death experience from a woman who went to Heaven. During her life review, although those in Heaven were very concerned about how she treated her partner, they were not at all concerned about the fact that she was a lesbian. The issue was never even brought up. Later I read a testimony from a gay man who was being guided to Heaven by three spiritual beings. He was quite concerned and worried about the fact that he had been a homosexual on Earth, and finally asked the angels who were with him, "Is it okay to be gay?" They laughed responding, "Who do you think made gay people?" I now have in my possession over 33 written and video testimonies from gay and lesbian people who went to Heaven. There is even a book by Liz Dale called "Crossing Over & Coming Home" that details the testimonies of gay and lesbian people who have had near-death experiences and went to Heaven.

These bodies are only shells that our spirits occupy. And although we may have our sexual identity with us in the lower levels of Heaven, at the core of who we are there is no sexual designation or orientation. Some souls may have dominant characteristics that we define as masculine or feminine qualities, but all those qualities are contained within the entirety of who God is. Claiming a person is somehow evil because of the particular shell they are occupying is just as silly as claiming a person is evil for driving a red car instead of a blue one. The body is just a shell that we are temporarily occupying. There is no shame or embarrassment in your choice of a romantic partner based on who you find attractive, whether same-sex or opposite. There is NO WRONGDOING in being gay. God made you just the way you are, and you should celebrate this!

There may be some in the lesbian, gay, bisexual, and transgender (LGBT) community who with good reason, may become bitter or angry towards those who condemn them. As someone who formerly judged and condemned the LGBT community, I would like to point out that I was not an evil person. I was simply spiritually immature and had been misled by my religion. If you are sitting in a restaurant and a man walks by and grabs your wallet, you might become angry. But what if a two-year-old child did it? Most people would be only slightly angry or mildly irritated. I would encourage all those in the LGBT community to view those who hate them not as bad people, but as people who are spiritually unaware. And the spiritually unaware need our caring, compassion and healing love, not more hatred. Those who criticize the LGBT community are mostly acting out of fear and ignorance. If they had any idea how damaging their hatred was for both themselves and the targets of their hatred, they would never hold onto such negative attitudes.

I remember the moment that my perspective towards the LGBT community changed. I was at an art and music festival attended by thousands of people. One man was standing in the street where there was a significant amount of pedestrian traffic, and was hugging people and kissing them on the cheek as they walked by. I don't know if he was gay or straight, on drugs or clean and sober, but this was not the issue. Being slightly homophobic and uncomfortable with the idea of receiving affection from another man, I attempted to avoid eye contact with him and walk right by. But he approached me without saying a word, smiled, hugged me, kissed me on the cheek, and then continued his gifting of affections to others. As I was walking away feeling a little creeped out, a very strong feeling of loving acceptance came into my heart, and I suddenly realized that such a display of unconditional love from any human being, man or woman, gay or straight, is a beautiful thing to be cherished and appreciated. And from that moment on my eyes were opened. I am grateful that I have learned to embrace all people regardless of their sexual orientation. It has made life easier for myself and for the people around me. And now I have a few very valuable friendships with gay men that I would have missed out on completely had I continued to hold onto my old judgmental concepts.

RELIGION VERSUS SCIENCE

There seems to be a universal idea that religion and science are diametrically opposed concepts. If one is right, the other must be wrong. But spirituality and science are actually one and the same. The problem is that we are simply not seeing the whole picture. If we did, there would be no perceived conflict between science and spirituality. Think of it like a magic trick. People are amazed and entertained by magic, not because there is anything incredible going on, but because of the perceived conflict. We know what the laws of physics are, and we know what is possible and what is impossible. A magic trick amazes us because we perceive the magician doing something that we know is impossible. But when the magician shows us how he did the trick, we are no longer amazed. We say, "Yes, of course. Now I see how it is done." The problem is not that the magician was breaking the laws of physics, but rather we did not understand everything that the magician was doing because we could not see the whole picture. Spirituality and science will someday merge, not because of compromise between the two, but because we will understand that the two sets of laws are really only one set. We just perceive a conflict where there is none because of our limited information and perspective. Science is nothing more than a way of describing the subset of the spiritual world that we call the physical world.

LOOKING FOR GOD

Since God is love, those of you who choose a religion in an effort to find God may be surprised at where your search eventually leads you. You will not find God confined to a mosque, a synagogue, or a cathedral. The answer to the question "Where is God?" cannot be answered because God is not in a *place*. When you find God, you will discover him in the only "place" where he can be found—in everyone and everything. For you personally, this means in your heart.

ADVICE ON RELIGION

People do not have the choice of where, what, and how to be born. If someone is a Christian or a Muslim or a Jew, I respect people on the basis of them being equal human beings. You have to accept the fact that there are other people who have different religious faiths. God does not choose between apples and oranges. He has created us all.

—Lily Habash, Executive Director,
Palestine Forum

If God relates to us and creates us in all our diversity,

then obviously there are unlimited ways of relating to God. You can never understand the totality of the divine because we are not God. And therefore, any religion is only a partial glimpse into that eternal truth, and none of us can have more than a partial glimpse.

— Chief Rabbi David Rosen

If you look just at the differences [in religions,] forgetting what the purpose is, there are big differences. But if you look at what is the purpose of these traditions, no matter how many differences there are, all carry the message of the importance of love, compassion, forgiveness, and tolerance. These are fundamental values of human beings. It becomes very clear; all these different philosophies are simply a different way of approach, but the same goal, the same message—to create a better human being.

— The Dalai Lama

We have a common humanity. We belong to different nations. We belong to different ethnic groups, and the religions also are different. But basically, we are all human. We have the same needs. We have the same aspirations, and we are faced with the same problems.

— Archbishop Michael Fitzgerald

As bees take honey from different flowers, similarly wise men take a sense of goodness from each and every religion.

— Rabbi Ezekiel Isaac Malekar

We have to go beyond the conventional approach to religion to get to the roots of these religions. We all share the one and only thing, which is peace and stability for all human beings, and free will for all humankind.

— Mohammad Khatami,
former President of Iran

I take this opportunity to thank all those, of whatever religion, who have sought to serve God, the God of peace, by building cities of brotherly love, by caring for our neighbors in need, by defending the dignity of God's gift, the gift of life in all its stages, and by defending the cause of the poor and the immigrant.

— Pope Francis
(Jorge Mario Bergogli)

God can be seen as a Tree of Life. And in this tree, there is a massive, beautiful, loving trunk with roots in the ground that connect all of humanity. The branches above spread out into many different religions—Hinduism, Islam, Christianity, Judaism, Buddhism, Catholicism, and many others, but the trunk is the core. Every single human being has the right to go their own direction and love God in their own way. You can honor God any way you want and still be part of the trunk. When we decide to love the man praying on the carpet as much as the man kneeling in the pew, it will dissolve the hatred that stems from the differences in our beliefs. Each religious person must learn to recognize God in others. Heaven does not care how you come to find the God inside you. They are not invested in the dynamics of religious structure as we are. The mind of God cannot be fathomed. It is not the mind of a human. It is pure compassion, light, and love. It does not have judgment. It does not have anger. It doesn't even have expectation. It simply loves. And this is what is inside you. Beautiful and honored is the human being who finds God in any organization and in any way with any doctrine![15]

HOW GOD VIEWS RELIGION

Imagine you have two young children that you adore. In a bitter divorce, your spouse gains custody of the children and out of spite moves far away and hides your children from you. You spend years searching for them, but finally give up in despair. Then one day years later your phone rings. It's your children. They tell you they were searching for you for many years and want to come and see you as soon as possible. They are in your neighborhood right now. Overflowing with emotion and excitement, you tell them to come over. You walk out to the street and anxiously await their arrival. After 10 minutes that seems like an eternity, a car comes driving down the street towards your house. It's them! Now, let me ask you a question—do you care what kind of car they are driving? Does it matter to you if it's a brand-new car in perfect condition or a broken-down old car with many problems? Of course not. You're just happy to finally see your children after all these years. God does not care how you come to him. Even if you are in a religion with many problems and questionable doctrines, God is overjoyed that you found him. It doesn't matter how you arrive. He will welcome you home with open arms.[16]

CHAPTER 6

EARTH, THE UNIVERSE, AND YOU

"You might sometimes feel alone in this world. You are not. Someone is watching over you and blessing your life, even though at times it may not seem like it."

— Movie: The Letter Writer

ANGELS AMONG US

All of Heaven works diligently to help us and there are more angels on Earth than there are people. For the purposes of this discussion, angels are all those spiritual entities of the light who directly interact with human beings to encourage and help us in positive ways. Angels interact with us in several ways. First, they speak directly to us, but because we are in a physical form, we cannot hear their words audibly. But we do hear them in the form of a thought in our heads.

Second, angels are able to "shine" emotions on us. For instance, if a man is angry with his brother, an angel may be sent who is a specialist with the emotion of compassion and forgiveness. The angel will shine a feeling of compassion and forgiveness on that man. This is not manipulation on the part of the angel, as it is always up to the individual to either accept or reject the angelic gift being offered. But more often than not the angels are successful in their efforts. If the man responds positively, he would contact his brother with an attitude of forgiveness and reconciliation.

Third, angels protect us both physically and spiritually. Angels can protect us from negative energies as well as prevent accidents from happening or reduce the injuries that occur during accidents. There would be far more accidents on Earth resulting in many more grave injuries if it were not for the intervention of angels protecting us. One example is a friend of mine who is an Episcopal priest. He was in a car accident, and his car rolled down a steep 200-foot embankment. He described being aware of a bubble of protection as the car was rolling. And although the car was completely destroyed, his only injury from the accident was a sprained ankle.

Fourth, angels are involved in answering prayers. They are assigned specific tasks from Heaven in direct response to our prayers here on Earth. The answer may not always be a direct granting of the request. For instance, a person who prays to win the lottery may have an angel sent to reveal that the nature of true happiness comes from seeking loving and meaningful relationships, not from excessive wealth. Near-death experiencers have been told that the angels are very eager to help us and are often willing to provide more help than God allows. Helping too much is counterproductive in the same way doing a child's homework for him would retard his learning process. Angels are restricted from helping us too much in order that we may grow and learn from our experiences here on Earth. If they do all of our homework for us, we won't learn our lessons as well.

Finally, angels make physical appearances, sometimes in angelic form, but more commonly masquerading as human beings or animals. These physical appearances are usually to assist people who are in desperate physical trauma and/or emotional turmoil. Recently I had the opportunity to see my best friend from grade school who I had not seen for 16 years. I remembered my friend Jerry as such a positive person—always happy, laughing, and easy-going. But when I saw him this time, he seemed grieved. I asked him how he was doing and if he was still married. For the first time ever, I saw my friend Jerry cry as he told me what he had been through in recent years. His wife of 26 years left him for a man who he thought was his friend, his business began failing, someone set fire to his apartment, his car was stolen, and he had been bitten by a venomous (brown recluse) spider that landed him in the hospital for three months, caused permanent chronic pain and left him with type one diabetes. During the worst day of his emotional distress, he went to a park thinking he was not going to make it through the day. Without knowing why, he walked up to a homeless man and offered him all the money in his wallet. The homeless man responded, "No, you keep it. I've been waiting for you." The homeless man started to talk to Jerry and encouraged him. He knew everything about Jerry; his name, his situation, and all the things he was going though. They spoke for hours, and it helped Jerry tremendously. Heaven sent Jerry help just when he needed it most.

PAUL THE FIREMAN

Genelle Guzman-McMillan worked as a secretary for the Port Authority of New York on the 64th floor of the World Trade Center's North Tower. On the day of the September 11, 2001, terrorist attacks, she was caught in the stairway of the 13th floor as the tower collapsed and 97 floors buried her in 30 feet of rubble. Only her left hand was free. Everything else was pinned down, and her head was stuck between two slabs of concrete. She spent the next 27 hours trapped and praying to God asking for a second chance at life. While she was praying, she started to hear trucks, mobile radios, and voices. She tried screaming but no one heard. Finally, she heard a voice. A firefighter reached through a hole in the rubble, gave her his hand, and offered her the comfort of his reassuring voice.

> He was talking to me and telling me I was going to be alright. He held my hand through it all. "I'm Paul," he said to me. "I'm here. Hang on. The rescuers are coming." It took a while for them to find me, but he never let go of my hand. He kept me calm. "Stay with me, stay with me." That's what he said.[17]

— Genelle Guzman-McMillan

It took about three and a half hours for firemen to dig her out. Genelle Guzman-McMillan was the last person alive to be rescued from the rubble. But when Genelle tried to find Paul to thank him, none of the firefighters knew anyone named Paul. Was Paul an angel sent from Heaven or perhaps even Paul the apostle? Probably.

DARK CITIES

If you've ever flown at night and looked out the window of the airplane, you can clearly distinguish the cities and their relative sizes from how brightly they shine. Uninhabited areas with little or no civilization appear dark. This is the exact opposite of how the Earth appears to near-death experiencers who see the Earth from space during their journey to the spiritual world. Every plant, animal, and human being gives off an aura of light. But because of our low level of spiritual development as a species, most human beings do not glow very brightly compared to plants. The pavement, buildings, and concrete that we construct in our cities glow very little if at all. So, when near-death experiencers look upon the Earth from space with their spiritual eyes, they see the parts of nature as being very bright and see dark areas where the cities are. One person reported a loud buzzing noise coming from some of the larger, darker cities.

WHY EARTH?

If you could experience, just for one day, what it is like to be a starving child living on the streets in a third world country, would you? In a manner of speaking, just by being here on this planet, you are doing just that. You are enduring a harsh and difficult environment as an experience of learning and growing. To truly appreciate peace, you must experience chaos. In order to truly appreciate unconditional love, you must experience fear and hatred. To appreciate bliss and ecstasy truly and profoundly, you must experience discomfort and pain. Part of the reason we are here is to learn an appreciation for the eternal inheritance we have received, and to learn that which we do not desire.

The question has come to my mind many times, why bother with Earth? It seems like such a difficult place to live, with so many problems and troubles. Why would a loving God put us in such a hostile environment? Why couldn't we just be born in Heaven and stay there permanently? I've never gotten a clear answer from near-death experiencers, but it seems to have something to do with learning certain lessons and developing spiritually. Our lessons are never punishments. Somehow suffering, hardship, and difficult challenges help us develop our souls and become better people.

Have you ever met someone who has suffered very few hardships during their lifetime? An example would be the son of a very wealthy person, or the child of a king. Not in all cases, but more often than not, those people who suffer and struggle very little during their lifetimes tend to be more self centered and less empathetic than those who have endured hardship and suffering. Although I am sure a few must exist, I have never met a homeless person who is arrogant and condescending. Mentally ill, yes, but seldom arrogant. Suffering somehow makes us better people and promotes humility.

THE KING'S SON

One analogy for potential benefits of an earthly life would be the story of the king's son. Once there was a good king who had a son who would one day rule his kingdom. The young prince grew up in the royal palace. He had servants and slaves to cater to his every whim and obey his every command. But the pampered lifestyle and position of authority led the young prince to grow up spoiled, egotistical, selfish, and have little compassion for the poor, and almost no concern for his subjects. The king realized that his son was unfit to be king. So, when the king had a second son, on the day he was born he brought his newborn son to a family of poor farmers and asked the family to raise his child as their own. They were never to reveal to the child that he was a prince. The prince grew up on the farm, learned to rely on his adopted family, and worked long, hard hours of backbreaking labor. Sometimes, when food was scarce, he went hungry. But other times when the situation was particularly bleak, the king would send his men during the night to leave food on the family's doorstep. So even though the young prince sometimes suffered and occasionally feared starvation, he was never in any danger because his father was secretly watching over him and protecting him. When the young prince became a man, the king came to the farm and revealed to him that he was a prince, and he would be crowned king one day. That young prince became a benevolent and humble king. He had compassion for the poor, love for his subjects, and was grateful for every royal meal he ate in the palace. He even said "please" and "thank you" to his servants.

The 1987 movie "Overboard" expresses this same concept in an entertaining way.

> "It's easier to be kind and loving to people who appreciate and thank you. A test of a man's character is how kind and loving he can be when no thanks, or even criticism, is given in return."

> *— Ron Suich, my father*

It's a lot tougher to be loving when you're having a bad day, or when you're suffering great physical or emotional pain. But just as a weightlifter's muscles need a weight heavy enough to stress their bodies, so our spirits need challenges that test the limits of our compassion and love. In this way we strengthen our spiritual muscles.

Although it's not exactly clear from a psychological standpoint why, somehow suffering and hardships make us better people. In many ways, we are like the king's second son. Often, we feel frightened here on Earth, as if we are abandoned and all alone. But we are never really in any danger. Just like the king in the story, our father, our family of light, is watching over us, making sure no harm will come to us, and covertly sending us help when we need it the most. And someday when you leave your earthly body and enter paradise, you will see that there was nothing to fear during this lifetime, because God was watching over you the whole time. You were never alone down here, not even for one second. You are safe, protected, and loved. Always.

THE BEGINNINGS OF LIFE

It's long been known that ancient Earth was pummeled by asteroids, meteors and comets that may have brought water and organic molecules to our planet and been responsible for the beginnings of life on Earth. Although there are many theories about how life on Earth began, the asteroid theory is correct. Near-death experiencers have been shown that planets are like eggs, and asteroids are like sperm. The asteroids bring organic life from other parts of the universe, depositing them on fertile planets. In this way life begins to evolve and proliferate on billions of different planets, and in billions of different ways. The process of creation is not over. It will grow and continue forever without end.

GETTING OLDER

As our scientists learn more about nature and the universe, the Earth keeps getting older. In the 1600s, Archbishop James Ussher of the Church of Ireland used the genealogies of Genesis to calculate the age of the earth at 6,000 years. Even modern science has a history of constantly revising upward their estimated age of the earth, our sun, and the universe. As a child I was taught that civilization began in Mesopotamia around 3,000 BC, but our historians now know that the Sumerians had large cities and advanced culture over 10,000 years ago. The truth is, there have been many civilizations on Earth long before modern humans, and many that are far older than 10,000 years. Many scientists approach the study of history with an attitude of arrogance and make the assumption that our society must be the most advanced civilization that has ever existed on Earth. In reality, some ancient civilizations possessed advanced technologies that we have lost. Many ancient cultures were also more spiritually advanced than we are, although we are a currently on a fast track to catch up and surpass all previous accomplishments.

GOD RECYCLES

In recent years, scientists have speculated that in the center of each galaxy lies a massive black hole. It was explained to one near-death experiencer that black holes are the universe's recycling machines, but unfortunately no further details were given.

A SIMPLE PLAN

During their near-death experiences, quite a few people were given a "download" of all the information that exists. After the download, they had no questions about anything because they knew all the answers. Unfortunately, when they returned to Earth, the immense amount of knowledge given to them could not be contained within a limited human brain. But all who were shown how the universe operates raved at the beautiful simplicity of it all.

> Suddenly... I knew all there was to know about everything. And I remember thinking how simple, how elegantly and unbelievably simple it all is; the whole system; life, everything. And I sat there in my non-body just contemplating the beauty of the utter simplicity of it.

> *— Neale, near-death experience*
> *during deep sleep*

INFINITY

> "Two things are infinite: the universe and human stupidity; and I'm not sure about the universe."

> *— Albert Einstein*

No matter how hard you try, you cannot possibly imagine how large our universe is. Let us consider the immense size of our known universe, forgetting about anything we know spiritually and just discussing what our scientists think they know. Our entire Milky Way Galaxy that contains over 300 billion stars is just a speck of light in the known universe. Traveling at the speed of light, roughly 670 million miles per hour, we could travel around the Earth seven times in one second. To cross our galaxy traveling at this tremendous rate of speed, we would have to travel 24 hours a day from birth till death, and then repeat that for 1200 lifetimes—just to cross the pinpoint of light in space that we call the Milky Way Galaxy. It is estimated there are at least 200 billion galaxies, all containing billions of stars. It is an unimaginably huge place.

The point is, if humans were alone in the universe, it would be way overbuilt. God isn't wasteful, so it should come as no surprise that when near-death experiencers ask God the very common question, "Are we alone in the universe?" the answer is always the same. The universe is full of life, and there are other dimensions with other universes that are also full of life. Believing that we are alone in the universe is just as ridiculous as mankind's past belief that the flat Earth was the center of the universe and everything revolved around us.

For a long time, I wasn't sure how many other dimensions there were. I suspected from string theory there might be 12 dimensions all containing universes of their own. But then one near-death experiencer stated he was shown the relative size of our entire universe in comparison to God's super-universe. He said that our entire universe appeared to be just a pinpoint in the super-universe of all that is. Apparently, God has a really big family, and we have lots of relatives.

STRING THEORY

String theory is a mathematical theory that tries to explain certain phenomena not currently explainable under the standard models of Newtonian and quantum physics. In string theory, the concept of traditional particle physics is replaced with a theory that all matter is made of strings of energy, each with its own unique energy signature and vibrational frequency.

There are several reasons why I suspect string theory is correct, although the "strings" vibrate in a circular or spherical manner as opposed to linearly as the name would imply. First, many near-death experiencers speak of vibrational energies in the spiritual world. There are indications that the soul is made of a light-love energy vibrating at a high frequency. The more advanced spiritual beings vibrate with higher frequencies and emanate higher energy levels. Second, (although this may not be part of known string theory on Earth) part of an object's specific energy signature and frequency determines the location of that object. Those species who possess the technology to travel interstellar distances that would be impossible at light speed, do so not by traveling faster than light, but by changing the portion of the energy signature of their ships that determines its location. In doing so their spaceships cease to exist in one place and instantaneously exist in another place according to how the energy signature is changed. They can literally change their spaceships into pure energy (sometimes referred to as "null space") and then convert that energy back into matter at a different location. Their ships can instantaneously "jump" distances that would take billions of years to travel at light speed.

VIOLENT SAVAGES

If you believe what the movies tell us about aliens, you know that they are all violent savages using highly advanced technology to do everything from stripping the Earth of its natural resources to consuming humans as a food source. Unfortunately, in comparison to most intelligent species in our galaxy, we are the violent savages, not them. In terms of technological and spiritual advancement, Earth is very low on the totem pole; we came late to the party with the development of intelligent life on our planet. By the time humanity had developed as a species, many other species of intelligent life elsewhere in the universe had millions of years of evolution, civilization, and technology. Long before the first single-cell organisms developed on Earth, species on other planets had already gone through the long process of spiritual ascension and were living in utopian societies of spiritual enlightenment and love. From their perspective, Earth is the kind of neighborhood that when you drive through it, you lock your car doors.

Although not all intelligent life in our universe is benevolent, many other species are well aware of the existence of God. These species live in peaceful and utopian societies where violence and crime do not exist. Some have even developed to the point where negative emotions such as fear, anger, and hatred have been forever eliminated from their range of emotions. For many species, the concept of creating a handheld device that shoots a metal projectile with the intent of injuring or killing another living being is insanely barbaric. Even worse than guns (to these beings) is the fact that we developed space travel and nuclear weapons during the same time period in our history. Those species who have been watching us were very concerned that we were going to destroy ourselves before having the opportunity to become a productive member of the galactic community. The reason for this is that every planet in the universe with intelligent life takes one of two paths; they either allow their fear and competition to dominate their cultures and eventually destroy themselves through war or environmental disasters, or they learn to live in harmony with their environment and each other, and advance both technologically and spiritually.

PEACE ON EARTH

Earth is on the latter path, thanks to a lot of help from above. Although it may not seem like it today, we have already passed the point of no return and are progressing towards a peaceful, utopian society that will be ruled by love. It won't quite be like Heaven, but compared to today's cultures of greed, domination, and violence, it will seem like Heaven on Earth. I will say this again to make it very clear as I have been shown this various times from multiple sources. **There will be no more world wars, no sudden mass extinction of human beings, and no Armageddon**. There will be peace on Earth, but it won't come gracefully. Dark forces will fight against their own inevitable demise with every last fiber of their strength, but they will lose because light is hundreds of times more powerful than darkness. The spiritual evolution and ascension of human consciousness is an accelerating juggernaut that can no longer be stopped. The game is over. The race has been won. From this point on, it is only a matter of the plan working itself out.

On this future Earth, humans will communicate telepathically with each other and with species on other planets. Large, populated cities will be replaced by small communities consisting of several hundred people who focus most of their energy on teaching children about love, art, music, nature, and God. There will be very little technology as it exists today. Manufacturing will exist, but it will be fairly limited due to mankind's new non-materialistic nature. Doctors will not be needed because any sickness will be healed by the collective consciousness and prayers of the community. Man will live in perfect harmony with each other and with nature. According to near-death experiencers, this will be accomplished within the next several hundred years. Despite the doom and gloom negativity that dominates mainstream media and thought patterns, the Earth and humanity are actually playing out an elegantly beautiful success story. And like most success stories, there are lots of minor and some major setbacks. But again, we have already passed the point of no return. Humanity is on an irreversible course towards spiritual ascension.

THE AMAZING LIBRARY OF GAIA

Compared to most other planets, Earth has a very wide variety of plant and animal life. Some alien planets are dominated by just two or three species and don't have the diversity of life that Earth enjoys. There are some planets where the weather is so moderate that the beings who live there have no need for buildings or dwellings for protection against the elements. There are other planets where entire civilizations live under water, and some planets filled with intelligent flying beings.

Earth was not some random act of nature as many of our scientists believe. It was actually planned and created by God and a whole host of God's helpers. There is no conflict between evolution and intelligent design, as the two are working hand-in-hand in the creation and evolution of every planet with life. Earth was designed as a free-will zone and a type of intergalactic genetic library. It is often referred to by other species as The Living Library.

Just as human beings are powerful spiritual beings inhabiting human bodies, Earth has a group of powerful spiritual beings inhabiting it. We call this collective feminine spirit Mother Nature, but her akashic name is Gaia. She is well aware of human beings and might be grieved by the harm we are doing to her as well as the lack of respect we are showing to the planet and the life on it. We act as if we own the entire Earth, but in reality, we are only temporary guests. Just as a patient parent puts up with an unruly teenager going through adolescence, our Mother Gaia is being patient with human beings as we mature spiritually. She is healing the wounds we inflict upon her, beautifying areas we devastate, and assisting us through our maturing process. But there is no need to worry—Gaia is far more resilient than our scientists believe, and she can heal all wounds caused by man. When humanity starts cooperating with nature and ceases polluting, our scientists will be shocked by how fast the Earth will heal.

A HARSH AND CHALLENGING ENVIRONMENT

In the spirit world you can sense the emotions and hear the thoughts of other beings. As some near-death experiencers are being guided towards Heaven by their spiritual guides, they sense feelings emanating from them. They report the angels' perspective of us as being very brave, like battle-hardened soldiers who have survived a long, harsh war. Compared to the average planet in our galaxy, Earth is a very difficult place to live. The physical environment is harsh, and there is a great deal of cruelty and violence. Although this is no longer the norm, many people on Earth are still operating in a fear-based survival mode and creating misery in the lives of others. Many near-death experiencers are shown that every person on Earth is a brave soul who has taken on a challenge so daring that few angels would even contemplate it. To those on the other side, we are the courageous ones. Make no mistake—the fact that you are here on this planet means you have taken on the granddaddy of all challenges—the Mount Everest of physical incarnations. Earth is one of the most difficult places to live in the entire galaxy.

WE ARE BEING WATCHED

At this moment, all eyes in the galaxy are upon us. In the history of our galaxy, no species has ever sunk so deep into negativity and darkness and then rebounded towards the light. Such an act, in spiritual terms, can be compared to pointing a bow and arrow upwards towards the sky and pulling back on the bowstring as far as possible. The further the bowstring is pulled back, the higher the arrow will go. The rest of the galaxy have watched us in disbelief and awe as we sunk further into darkness than was ever done before, and then sprang out into the light. The arrow in our analogy is the consciousness of love and the very essence of God. Our galactic brothers and sisters, without having to go through the trauma of dipping so far into the darkness we experienced, are learning from our example. By what we have done and are still doing, we are elevating all life in our galaxy. Our particular specialty is compassion, which is the highest possible vibrational expression of love on this planet. Even those in Heaven learn and elevate their consciousness because of our activities and the work we do here.

When you wake up in the morning and see yourself in the mirror, do not just think of yourself as an average person going through the routines of each day, working, paying your taxes, and going out on the weekends. If you are here on this planet during this exciting time, you are an amazing and brave soul, working diligently to uplift all of creation!

THE SOUL'S NATURE

I debated for a long time whether I should include the following topic in this book. My biggest fear was that people would mentally throw out the baby with the bathwater. But I decided I would not go down the same road the Catholic Church did over 500 years ago. As much as this idea may bother some people, I refuse to conceal the truth I have learned. During the Council of Trent many decisions were made that form today's modern Bible. One near-death experiencer was shown the history of the Bible's creation, and the Catholic Church's decision to exclude certain spiritual knowledge they deemed inappropriate for the public. One issue the Church decided to conceal was that of multiple lifetimes, and those scriptures containing such information were omitted. Luckily for us, they overlooked one verse. In Matthew 11:14, Jesus said, "And if you are willing to accept it, John the Baptist himself is Elijah who was to come."

I was very disturbed the first few times I heard near-death experiencers describe seeing other lifetimes during their life reviews. But the evidence became too overwhelming to deny, and I have now come to accept the fact that as souls we do not have just one physical incarnation in a single lifetime, but many different lifetimes on many planets, not just Earth. This process is far different than the traditional perception of reincarnation as one lifetime after another with no activity in between and no connection between physical incarnations. The reality of multiple lives is much different and more exciting than that! As souls, we are multidimensional beings actually living multiple lives simultaneously, outside the dimension of time. And just as we sometimes enjoy reading a book or watching a movie to experience a different reality, our souls enjoy incarnating into physical existences to experience different realities. Part of the reality of physical existence on this planet is amnesia. We have forgotten other lifetimes and our Heavenly origin, but not completely, causing some people to feel out of place. If you've ever felt like you don't belong, it is because Earth is not your home, but rather a temporary adventure far from home. And as fun and exciting as this adventure may be, many of us do sometimes get homesick.

Multiple lifetimes doesn't mean one lifetime after another with no connection, but rather from an eternal perspective, we choose to experience various lives, which can often appear like the blink of an eye compared to our eternal nature. Souls prepare themselves to come to Earth, and some near-death experiencers have even described being assisted by their spiritual guides in choosing a life and their parents. From our perspective, we have already lived all our past lifetimes, and have yet to choose future lifetimes. However, from our souls' perspective, all lifetimes are happening simultaneously. Each physical life affects the person's soul or higher self, and correspondingly the higher self affects every single lifetime. For example, if you really dislike cold weather it might just be a product of your particular biology, or you may have lived another lifetime during an ice age where you were cold the entire time. Many personality traits, fears, likes, dislikes, and talents come from our multidimensional selves and other lives. This multidimensional existence may soon receive some validation from the scientific community, as they will eventually discover that our DNA has a quantum nature to it that exists outside of three-dimensional time and space. When our scientists develop ways to measure different quantum energies, they will begin to discover there is far more to existence than we previously believed.

OLD SOULS

Our first lifetimes are typically lived on planets where the inhabitants are already spiritually advanced. Younger souls require safer, less hostile environments, until they are ready for bigger and more exciting challenges. You would never send a child who just learned to walk on a trek up Mount Everest. Similarly, the souls here on Earth are mostly older, more experienced souls. As Earth is an extremely challenging environment, it takes an older and more experienced soul to properly manage the fear and love duality of our earthly existences. If you are here now reading these words, you have already experienced many lifetimes. You have been short, tall, heavy, thin, gay, straight, good-looking, and homely. You have given birth and fought on the battlefield. You have died in different ways, by every natural means possible, and by various acts of violence. Any situation you can think of, you've probably already gone through it. You have experienced life as a human of many different races, practicing different religions, and living all over the world. Some near-death experiencers report being aware of hundreds of earthly lifetimes, as well as lifetimes on other planets. In temporal terms, the average human being may have a soul that is well over one million years old. But this is deceptive, as there is no time on the other side of the veil. In a sense, you are immortal, and you always have been. Simply put, you are as eternal as God because you are part of God. You have always existed, and you always will.

Did you know that the souls on this planet all know each other on the other side of the veil? We are a family, and we have been together for a very long time. Did you know that together we watched the creation of this Universe and helped our Father build it? We did. You are much more than you have been led to believe.

WHO WE ARE

There have been many masters who came to Earth to show us the way: Jesus, Buddha, Mohammed, and others. As human beings we tend to elevate them to the status of a deity. In a sense, that is a valid perspective. The newly sprouted sapling that has barely broken the soil might look at the mighty oak and see God. The sapling is inferior in many ways. Just one strong rainstorm and the sapling washes away, but the mighty oak stands up against floods and storms. Is the sapling inferior to the oak, or just at a different stage of its development? The masters who came to teach us were not trying to elevate themselves to the position of God. They were trying to show us the God in everyone. They were attempting to teach us what we are capable of becoming.

One of the reasons that God loves you so much is because you are a part of him. God could not dislike you any more than you could dislike your own heart, lungs, and limbs. Not only do you appreciate them, you absolutely need them as a functioning part of who you are. You are far more necessary to God than your hands and feet are to you. A person could survive without hands or feet, but if only one soul, just one tiny portion of God's creation were to cease to exist, all of creation would break down and cease. The entire machine would stop. THAT is how important you are! You may be a very tiny gear in the machine of the trillions of intelligent beings that are all expressions of God, but if that tiny gear breaks the whole machine breaks down. Of course, that would be impossible because no part of God is capable of non-existence. Nevertheless, no one can do the job that you do. No one else in the entire existence of creation brings the unique and valuable expression of love that is you. If you've ever had anyone tell you that you are special, they really had no idea of what an understatement that is.

> We would have you understand that the flame that you are burns eternally and shall never go out, no matter how bright you allow yourself to become. We shall have you understand that you exist now, and always shall and you always have, because now is the only time and the only place and the only existence there is, and always has been, and ever shall be. You are eternal. You are infinite. You are spirit. You are body. You are mind. You are heart. You are soul. You are an idea. You are an expression. You are a thought. You are a dream of the infinite creation. But that is reality, and all reality is couched within your dream. You contain it all. You are the whole expression in your own individualized way. You are the matrix. The matrix is you. You are everything. Everything comes from you. Everything gives birth to you as you reinforce the existence of everything and everyone. All that is, the infinite creation, the fabric of existence chose you—chose that you should exist! It chose you, consciously chose you. You are in that way therefore blessed, and we would have you understand that simply because of the fact that you exist, you are blessed. For you are created out of divine material, out of divine life. You are the infinite creator. And your existence was a conscious decision, a conscious thing, a conscious choice. Act in like manner. Be of like mind. Respect yourselves. Love yourselves

unconditionally, for out of unconditional love were you created, and out of unconditional love shall you create anything you desire. Begin to feel the energy of your interlinking with all thought forms. All consciousness, all civilization, all ideas, all minds, all hearts, all souls, all spirit is one. And you are one within that seed, within that pool. Know that you are the fabric and the essence of the galactic energy. Not one of you in that sense can be removed from the matrix without the collapse of the entire structure. You are integral in that way. You are essential in that way. And we would have you understand that because you are interconnected in this way, because everything you do has impact within the entirety of creation, that you deserve to exist in this way, and that you deserve to be the fullest individual that you can imagine yourself to be, that you deserve to manifest all the things that you can conceive of, that you deserve the existence you have been given or it would not have been granted to you, that you deserve all the love that you can imagine because love is what you are made out of, that you deserve all the light that you can create in your life, because light is what you are made out of. Feel in the beating of your heart that it keeps pace with the rhythm and the pulse of the spinning of all the galaxies, of the fabric of existence itself, of the universal heart of infinite creation. For you all beat within that heart, and not one of you is outside of the heart of all that is. You are the blood and the life force of God himself. It is your force and your life as well. You are it and it is you. Out of your dreams, be born. Out of your heart, be alive. Out of your soul, be light, for you are nothing else.[18]

— Bashar (Darryl Anka)

CHAPTER 7

PEACE AND LOVE

"Love covers a multitude of sins."

— Paul the Apostle,
1 Peter 4:8

The Bible mentions love over 500 times. Love is supreme. It is the all-important overlying force that creates the universe and connects us all together. Love is the very substance and essence of who God is and what he is made of. When we talk about love, we are not talking about an emotion or a feeling, but a being, a benevolent source of life and light, the source of all that is, and the source of who we are. If you live your life with love, you are living your life with God because God IS love. It is impossible to be a godly person without being a loving person, and it is impossible to be a loving person without being a godly person, because God and love are one and the same—the two cannot be separated.

A BACKWARDS PHILOSOPHY

One of the most important lessons in my life is that almost everything I was brought up to believe turns out to be untrue. Now I don't blame my parents for this, in fact I don't blame anyone for this. They, just like everybody else, were brought up with the same founding, justifying, centralizing myths. All classes have them. All groups of people subscribe to them, and they're always wrong.[19]

— George Monbiot,
BBC Journalist and political activist

Beginning during our youth we are taught to be independent, self-sufficient, and compete for the things that we need including love. People go to great extremes "looking for love." They are set against each other to compete for everything, from a job needed for survival to a mate for creating a family. Even the system of money itself, an extremely useful tool for exchanging goods and services, encourages a person to work for themselves out of self-serving necessity rather than contributing to the community as a whole out of love. The entire human race has embraced a philosophy of backwards fear-based competition rather than love-based cooperation.

A perfect example is the way Hollywood portrays a person pursuing happiness. Movies often show the main character struggling to achieve happiness, peace, and find that perfect romantic partner to complete the fantasy. This backwards philosophy is so ingrained into our culture that we think it is normal. Unfortunately, it is contrary to the spiritual laws of nature.

When does a person feel love? If somebody you despise loves you, do you feel anything? Usually not. You only feel love when you are *expressing* love to another. If you want peace, you don't go out looking for that perfect set of circumstances that will give you peace. You have to create an environment of peace for others. If you want love, you have to love others without judgment or reserve. The true pursuit of happiness (an expression of love) involves each individual embracing and becoming the change they wish to see in others. If you want to be treated with kindness and compassion, then be kind and compassionate to the people around you, especially when your ego tells you they do not deserve it. If you want an abundance of love in your life, then pour out an abundance of love for the people around you and perform random acts of kindness whenever opportunities arise. You will be amazed how well this works and how much it will enrich your life and the lives of the people around you. The old biblical principle of "whatsoever a man soweth, that shall he also reap" is not some threat of punishment for breaking God's rules, but a universal spiritual law that is always in place and active. Simply stated, whatever you focus your energy on will be manifested in one form or another.

We live in a world where there is constant competition for resources among people, businesses, economies, governments, and countries. Thankfully, not only is love an inexhaustible resource, but it multiplies with use. Imagine if you were given two dollars for every dollar you spent for as long as you live. The more you tried to spend, the richer you would become. That is the way love works. When you give love, it multiplies exponentially, and everybody wins. Near-death experiencers have been shown that one person living in perfect unconditional love is more powerful than millions living in fear and doubt.

ROMANTIC LOVE

In our culture when someone speaks of love it is usually associated with romantic love. When someone says, "I'm looking for love," you wouldn't think they were looking for meaningful friendships. But romantic love often starts as a self-serving love. People are looking to be loved rather than to give unconditional love to another. In other words, love as viewed by our culture often has a selfish motive. But true love is given expecting nothing in return. When a person speaks about being "in love," they are actually referring to an altered emotional state of ecstasy that comes from perceiving their partner from a perspective of unconditional love, and experiencing being loved unconditionally in return. But this state of bliss does not require a romantic relationship.

AN ALTERED STATE

"Love is at the root of everything—all learning, all parenting, all relationships. Love, or the lack of it."

— Fred McFeely Rogers (Mr. Rogers)

I have heard people talk about an altered state of consciousness, and I have experienced that state of unconditional love. It is a feeling of happiness, bliss, and peace; a comfort that everything is as it should be. It also carries with it a feeling of connectedness, of being part of everything and everyone, like a giant extended family. But this bliss, this altered state of consciousness, is not an "altered" state at all. It is actually our normal state of being. The state of consciousness of fear, pain, anger, jealousy, and strife is the unnatural altered state of consciousness that affects human beings who are operating principally out of fear. Sadly, many people unknowingly suffer in this altered unnatural state of consciousness for much of their lives.

CREATING UTOPIA

"The more we tried to make our lives simple, the more complex they became, and now the son of man is sentenced to 10 to 15 years of school just to survive in this complex and hazardous environment that we have created."

— From the movie,
The Gods Must be Crazy

We tried to make things perfect for ourselves. In the United States we have over 180,000 pages of federal laws, not even counting thousands of state laws and rules from hundreds of regulatory agencies. We have made a valiant effort to create for ourselves a safe and peaceful utopia, but somehow it hasn't worked out as we had expected. Big government and big business don't seem to be contributing to our overall happiness, but detracting from our freedoms.

Creature comforts don't seem to have helped us much either. Today's technology and mass production have brought a tremendous amount of comforts, conveniences, and luxuries to the average person that were unattainable to the wealthiest royalty 200 years ago. No king of the past, regardless of how wealthy or how powerful he was, had what I have. I can communicate with millions of people around the world within a matter of seconds. From my home I can review and buy almost any product and get it delivered directly to my door a few days later. I can travel to any part of the world in less than 48 hours—something that would have taken months or years in the past. Even my transportation is amazing. It is fast, smooth, quiet, and temperature conditioned. It can create the sound of a symphony with no musicians present and has the power of 270 horses. Any king from the distant past would be truly amazed and envious of the things I can do and the places I can go.

We are by far the most comfortable and pampered generation in history. But are we also the happiest? Obviously, the comforts and conveniences that we so hoped would enrich our lives are just not producing the results we had anticipated. In many cases they are having the opposite effect. Plants, animals, people, and the Earth itself have all paid a tremendous price to bring us these luxuries, and they're not even making us any happier. Clearly, materialism is not the answer to true happiness. We live in a culture that has embraced materialism as a path to happiness, yet study after study has shown that after people's basic necessities have been met, additional wealth and luxuries do not increase a person's happiness. I have personally noticed that the more material possessions a person accumulates, and the nicer those possessions are, the more complicated and stressed that person's life becomes. Just look at some of the Hollywood actors. They have it all—fascinating and exciting careers, good looks, popularity, money, fame, and fortune. But they, like so many others who win the rat race, can end up becoming severely depressed or turning to drugs to fill the void in their hearts.

> While on earth, it would serve a person best not to work on attaining wealth, possessions, and physical beauty, but rather in developing such qualities as hope, faith, good works, love, patience, forgiveness, and charity. This is the light that emanates from a spirit being and truly shows what a person worked for and obtained while in mortality.
>
> — *Kim Rives, after her*
> *near-death experience*

One of the first and most important steps to filling your life with love is to take your focus off the things that distract you from your true purpose. Leave materialism behind. Buying lots of nice stuff is a fool's game for both the buyer and the seller. Admittedly, shedding material possessions is a very difficult proposition. Society, corporations, and the media have pounded the message into our heads since birth that our happiness depends on whatever thing they happen to be pushing at the moment. We did not come to this planet to press buttons on a smartphone or go on shopping sprees. When you shed material possessions you will see how much fulfillment love for people (as opposed to things) brings.

> "Only a life lived for others is worth living."
>
> — *Albert Einstein*

At the end of a person's life, does anybody regret not having bought more stuff? Have you ever heard a person who is dying say with their final breath, "I wish I would have spent more time at the office," or "I wish I would have bought nicer things"? Of course not. A focus on loving, meaningful relationships is what fulfills a person's life, and when that life ends, they know this. They want to be surrounded by the people they love, not by the material possessions they acquired.

FEAR-BASED LIVING

You don't have to look far to see that we are living in a world of disharmony. We seem to be plagued by selfishness, corporate greed, government corruption, financial crises, environmental disasters, terrorism, and wars. Governments, mega-corporations, and central bankers have hoarded power and wealth at such an alarming rate as to severely oppress the very human beings they were created to serve in the first place. Wealth and income inequality have skyrocketed to the point that a few hundred people control more wealth than the rest of the world combined; meanwhile common workers' wages have stagnated. We have created a worldwide culture where money and profit have first priority, even over human life itself. And when you make money your number-one priority, everything else suffers—families, children, communities, workers, and the environment. The global economy continues to encourage an ever increasing and unsustainable level of production and consumption. And unfortunately, any society dedicated to consumerism ultimately consumes and extinguishes itself. This is not our path.

Many of the super wealthy are living in tremendous fear. No sane person would continue to focus on accumulating wealth when they have more money than they could ever spend in a dozen lifetimes. Fear-based living causes people to make all sorts of poor decisions and creates problems for themselves and for the people around them. The ruling elite are a perfect example of fear-based living. They mistakenly associate their wealth with happiness and are very concerned about maintaining the status quo. Thus, they are constantly trying to strengthen their financial positions at the expense of everyone else. They are very fearful that those whom they oppress could gain equality or, even worse, the upper hand. Economies will have to change and be managed for the benefit of people instead of the competitive money sport that they have become.

LEAVING FEAR BEHIND

"Security is mostly a superstition. It does not exist in nature, nor do the children of men as a whole experience it. Avoiding danger is no safer in the long run than outright exposure. Life is either a daring adventure or nothing."

— Helen Keller

"You must realize that fear is not real. It is a product of thoughts you create. Danger is very real, but fear is a choice."

— From the movie: After Earth (2013)

Fear is a lack of awareness of love, a flaw in perception, and does not exist in reality. Fear is also imagining an undesirable future scenario that does not currently exist in the present moment, and in most cases never exists. A person who says they have a fear of flying does not actually fear flying. What they fear is the imagined scenario of the plane crashing and the end to their existence.

Since fear is the opposite of love, part of the process of growing and maturing spiritually is learning to overcome fear. Recognizing that you are immortal is a big step. Any situation, no matter how dismal it may seem in the moment, is temporary and will last only the blink of an eye compared to the eternity you are living.

Fear-based living tricks humans into believing that we must fight each other to survive. This is not our nature. The force of love inspires us to cooperate with each other, rather than to compete with each other, and the efficiencies that result are astounding.

At the time this book was written we had 3.5 million homeless people in United States, and 18.5 million vacant homes; meaning vacant homes outnumber homeless people by over 5 to one. If the United States were to take just 10% of our military budget and devote it to the homeless, it would provide over $15,000 per homeless person per year. What we have is a resource distribution problem, not a resource scarcity problem. The human race has already built more than enough housing for every human being on earth, but millions of homes remain vacant while millions of people have no home. We are so focused on competition and deciding who gets paid for what that we are blind to the fact of how much waste our competition creates. Some will undoubtedly argue that we will never be able to convince people to build a house and not get paid for it. The Amish have been doing just that as part of their culture. Charities have been providing housing for the poor for hundreds of years.

We must abandon this dangerous notion that labor can be given only in exchange for money. The human race is already producing enough food, clothing, medicine, and housing to care for all of humanity—even those who are too old, sick, or weak to care for themselves. If we are to advance as a species, we must release our fear, and embrace the cooperation that comes with love for all.

I AM YOU

> "Look around for the hidden messages of beauty and truth. You can find them in every tree, every flower, and every human being. We are all connected, along for each other's encouragement, understanding, and love."

— From the Movie: The Letter Writer

The connection of people and all living things is a recurring theme in this book because of its importance in the way we relate to each other. If you imagine the entire ocean as God, you can look at yourself as a drop of water in that ocean. Every drop of water in the ocean experiences from a unique perspective what it is like to be that tiny part of the ocean. Some drops are in the arctic cold, others are in warm tropical waters, and some drops experience evaporation, returning to the ocean when it rains. Each drop of the ocean has a unique experience of being a drop of water in the ocean. Similarly, each human being experiences a different reality because of their unique perspective and experiences. A rickshaw driver in China and a lumberjack in Oregon will experience two completely different perspectives of reality during the same day, with almost nothing in common. In each moment of your life, no single person or creature in the entire universe is experiencing your perspective of reality. The things you are saying, feeling, seeing, and doing are unique to the experience you are living in the moment.

Now let's take this one step further. I have some evidence from near-death experiencers that the following analogy may be quite accurate; Let us imagine that God can be compared to a giant crystal plate that shatters into trillions of pieces. Some pieces might be quite large and comprise 20 or 30 percent of the entire plate, and other pieces might be microscopic dust-sized particles. But each piece of the plate is a unique and necessary part of the plate as a whole. God is the whole plate, and each one of us is a small but necessary piece. When you look at another person, you are actually looking at a different piece of yourself, the same you, a piece of the crystal plate, but experiencing it from a different perspective of reality.

Every person out there, every child, every driver on the road, every person you meet—they are all you, and they are all part of God. I find it a lot easier to treat other people lovingly when I recognize the magnificence of who they are. They are me, and I am them, and they are part of all that is, the whole being of God. We are each a unique and precious expression of one universal being. Part of humanity's process through spiritual ascension includes learning to see God in everything and everyone, including yourself. You have heard the saying *God is Great*. Yes, you certainly are!

It's hard to believe, isn't it? That in a sense you are God in the same way that a drop of ocean water is the ocean. It's true. Why else would God call us his children? We are part of each other—a family of light; united but experiencing a temporary illusion of separateness for the purposes of enjoyment, learning, and consciousness expansion.

THE REAL INTERNET

> "Love is the basic principle of how everything works. You don't cause pain, you don't do violence to anything in any way, even in the subtlest way, because it hurts the whole system."
>
> *— From the movie: I AM, by Tom Shadyac*

All life, everything and everywhere, is connected at all times through a universal energy field. I am not just talking about spiritual energy or chakras or auras, but an actual measurable energy field. The HeartMath Institute, an organization dedicated to studying the science of the heart, did an experiment where they placed very sensitive electrodes to a culture of bacteria contained within a Petri dish of yogurt. The electrodes can sense minute changes in the electromagnetic field produced by the bacteria. When a person is sitting within a few feet of the yogurt, but not connected to the yogurt in any way, the changes in their emotional state show up in the form of electromagnetic signals in the yogurt. The HeartMath Institute isn't exactly sure why this happens, but it does prove that we are connected in a deep way that science does not yet fully understand. The heart produces an electromagnetic field that can be measured as far as 12 feet away. The HeartMath Institute has shown through experimentation that the heart's interstitial beats (the space between heartbeats) change according to a person's emotional state. Furthermore, they have shown that when two people are close to each other, not only can each person sense the other's heartbeat, but also the proximity of the hearts to each other causes physiological effects. So just by your emotional state you are putting out an electromagnetic signal that affects other people.

Have you ever been in a public place and been standing next to a stranger, and without exchanging any words, for some reason that person just gives you the creeps? Or alternatively, have you ever met someone, and before they even speak a word you feel comfortable and safe with that person? That is your heart sensing the emotional state of their heart, either through this electromagnetic field that we can measure and interpret, or by some other unknown means.

When I was a child, my mother got a phone call at 2 o'clock in the morning from the hospital because my grandfather suffered a pancreatic attack. But the phone call didn't wake her up. Although she was usually a very sound sleeper, she had been unable to fall asleep, and was restless and unsettled most of the night. When she called my aunt to give her the bad news, before she could tell her what happened, my aunt asked, "What's wrong with Dad?" Somehow, my mother and my aunt knew that my grandfather was in crisis. This is not uncommon. If you ask around, you will find that most people have either had this experience themselves or know somebody that had a similar experience.

EVERY DAY, YOU CHANGE THE WORLD

> Making a difference is not about a project. It's the way you show up in the world every single day. You are already making a difference whether you know it or not, whether you like it or not. Just by your presence—your vibrational presence, is always making a difference. You made a difference today to everyone who saw you, felt you, or heard you. So, the question then is, what kind of difference am I making? Don't measure it in terms of money. Don't measure it in terms of fame. Don't measure it in terms of even how many people you've affected. Shifting one person is sacred.
>
> — *Dr. Barbara De Angelis*

Many near-death experiencers have come back from Heaven with the knowledge of how important words and thoughts are. They say things like, "If I had known how powerful my words and thoughts were, I would have paid much more attention to my thought processes and the things I said."

Every word you speak to another human being has an effect, and that effect—positive or negative—is felt throughout the entire planet. Your thoughts, words, and emotions affect the entire Earth including every plant, animal, and human being. If people were capable of fully understanding the nature of God and our connection with the divine, not a single human being would speak an unkind word to another. The very idea would be repulsive.

Even the smallest act of kindness can bring the greatest joy, and just one good deed is worth a thousand prayers. Many near-death experiencers have said they were shown in Heaven that just one random act of kindness elevates all of humanity. This results from the increase in a higher vibrational energy that your soul takes on. This energy change—however small it may be—affects the entire human race through our common connection. And assuming the recipient of your act of kindness responds in a positive manner, his increase in positive vibrational energy will be felt throughout the Earth as well. When you bring hope or joy to just one soul, millions receive the vibration.

TAKING CONTROL

Knowing that your emotional state and your personal daily activities can affect everyone on Earth, this would probably be a good time to talk about learning to direct your thoughts and feelings. The vast majority of people go through each day in a normal routine, paying very little attention to their thought processes. Essentially, they let their thoughts run wild in whatever direction their brain's subconscious decides to take them. But if you decide to start paying attention to your thoughts, and when you start to think negative thoughts, critical thoughts, judgmental thoughts, or anything dark or fear-based, stop yourself!

As I look around this world, I see an ample amount of both beauty and horror. If I choose to focus on the beauty, that's what will dominate my thought processes. But if I choose to focus on everything that's wrong with the world, it will affect me negatively—and correspondingly the rest of the world in a negative way.

You can't single-handedly save the environment, but you can do your best to reduce waste and recycle. You can't eliminate corruption in business and politics, but you can decide on a personal level to act with honesty and integrity in everything you do. You cannot feed every hungry person in the world, but you can give one homeless person a meal. Whenever you feel moved in your heart to reach out and be kind to another, do it! It will benefit both you and the recipient of your random act of kindness. It is impossible to help another human being without helping yourself. The quickest way to change the world is to be of service to others.

I have difficulty watching most news, TV programs and movies. Avoiding these sources of toxic programming was a great benefit in helping my thinking process become more positive. Most news is a constant drumbeat of negativity, depression, and fear. Just go to any major news source and count how many negative versus positive news stories there are. The negative news usually dominates by 80% or more. News is essentially a well-crafted fear report. As an alternative to the regular news, I enjoy reading The Good News Network (www.goodnewsnetwork.org)

For spiritual development, it is best to just focus on your own world and the people around you. Do your best to be loving, kind, patient, and forgiving to the people you come in contact with during your daily activities. Don't worry about the rest of the world. Your good deeds will be felt in the vibrational network of energy connecting us all, and your positive contribution to the energy field will encourage others, on a soul level, to follow your example.

MOTHER EARTH

> "Our task must be to free ourselves by widening our circle of compassion to embrace all living creatures, and the whole of nature and its beauty."
>
> — *Albert Einstein*

As a species we share the Earth with many other plants and animals, yet we act as if we own the entire planet. The Earth is a gift to be shared by all life inhabiting it, not just human beings. Unfortunately, we are the only species dominating, controlling, and destroying nature instead of living in harmony with nature. I am very encouraged as I see more and more people moving in the right direction. Many people are building sustainable living structures, reducing waste, recycling, and focusing on caring for nature and the planet. We are on the right path! I applaud all those who are involved in this noble effort. Showing love and compassion for the Earth is just as necessary and critical as showing love for each other. If the Earth dies, we die. We must care for, and unconditionally love, our mother Gaia.

> Part of our responsibility as stewards of the Earth is to respect the design of nature. You can go down the line— avian flu, mad cow, salmonella, fisteria, campylobacter, e-coli, just go down the line, and every single one of these things is nature speaking to us today, screaming to our industrialized culture saying, enough!

> *— Joel Salatin, Sustainable Farmer,*
> *From the movie: Fresh*

Just as we have love for each other, God wants us to have love for nature and the Earth as well. As difficult and harmful as it may be to world economies, we must change our current way of living or it will be changed for us by force. Unrestrained growth and environmental abuse will have to end as part of our spiritual evolution, so we have no other choice than to reinvent our civilization in a way that is sustainable. We have to stop forced industrial farming and return to organic planting. We have to halt the unsustainable growth of production, consumption, and waste of manufactured products. Any animals that we use as food sources must not be sentenced to miserable existences just because it is more cost effective. Animals are sentient beings with feelings and emotions and must be treated as such. They are our relatives, not our property.

Through billions of years of experience, trial, and error, Mother

Nature has created a perfectly balanced self-sustaining ecosystem. She has far more experience than we do when it comes to running this planet. We need to *listen to her* and follow her example. That means no genetically modified foods, no agricultural chemicals, no artificial fertilizers, no artificial pesticides, no massive burning of fossil fuels, no strip mining, and no weapons tests that damage the environment. We must also eliminate a whole host of other activities that are damaging this planet. We must reject this dangerous concept that humans are separate from nature; We are part of it. But just as important as cooperating with Mother Nature, we must learn to cooperate with each other.

COOPERATION VERSUS COMPETITION

If you talk to people in aboriginal and indigenous cultures, you find that the highest societal value is cooperation, and competition has a very low value. And competition beyond certain boundaries is considered a mental illness. If you look at our culture, cooperation is considered a very low value, and competition is considered the highest value, and we celebrate the most powerful competitors.

— Tom Harmann, Author
from the movie: I AM

Our society is so focused on competition and celebrating the strongest competitors that even most of our games are based on competition. Human beings like to participate in competitive games because it's basically an opportunity to win and then declare, "I am better than the rest of you." In a way, it is almost a type of psychosis. On other planets, many of their games are centered around cooperation—but we celebrate one winner, or one winning team, while the losers are often sad or shamed. We have even had TV shows such as *Lifestyles of the Rich and Famous* that glorify those who have hoarded the most material possessions. And although competition in business has led to great leaps in efficiency and productivity, it has also led to competing through cheating as we see in much of corporate America today. All you have to do is listen to any consumer advocate on the radio to hear about all the underhanded games and fraudulent activities that businesses contrive to unfairly separate people from their money. False advertising, junk fees, counterfeit products, planned obsolescence, up-sells, and scams are commonplace in American businesses. Worse yet, competition between countries for resources, a dominant religion, or political power leads to economic battles and war.

WAR AND VIOLENCE

I am not here to make excuses for war or to justify war, but I definitely am not going to glorify war. War is death, disease, destruction, disablement, and a sheer waste of men and women and raw materials. The only people that profit from war are the men who make the munitions and the guns. Nobody wins wars. There are losers on every side.

— *World War II Veteran*

"Nothing will end war unless the people themselves refuse to go to war."

— *Albert Einstein*

All war must end. God has made it very clear to near-death experiencers that he wants us to find peaceful ways to work out our differences. In the short-term violence might temporarily function to subdue an enemy, but it never works in the long term. Iraq and Afghanistan are perfect examples. Bombing our way to peace is just as ridiculous as a person punching his way to friendship. It never works. The use of force and violence against another almost always has the undesired effect of escalating violence, and eventually leads to long-term hatred and resentment.

> Darkness cannot drive out darkness; only light can do that. Hate cannot drive out hate; only love can do that. Hate multiplies hate, violence multiplies violence, and toughness multiplies toughness, in a descending spiral of destruction. The chain reaction of evil must be broken, or we shall be plunged into the dark abyss of annihilation.

> *— Dr. Martin Luther King Jr.*

Imagine if the Department of Homeland Security announced to the people of the United States that they have identified terrorists and people who are a threat to our national security living within major US cities including Los Angeles, San Francisco, New York, Dallas, and Chicago. Furthermore, they state their plan is to use precision bombing and drones within our own cities to kill thousands of terrorists, but in the process, approximately 150,000 innocent men, women and children will die. Americans wouldn't stand for it—there would be mass protests in the streets. But somehow it was okay for us to do exactly that to the people of Iraq and Afghanistan. Are the lives of Iraqi and Afghan children any less valuable than the lives of American children? Of course not. However, to kill those who we perceive as threats we consider it a necessary sacrifice—a sacrifice we would never accept if it were our own children being slaughtered.

There will be people who read this section on war and immediately start justifying our behavior by pointing out that many countries are far more violent and ruthless than we are, or even saying that we are only defending ourselves. But as the old saying goes, two wrongs do not make a right. I use the behavior of 9/11 only as an example. The common reason reported for 9/11 was that Islamic radicals hated Americans, so they killed 3,000 people by flying planes into the Twin Towers. Then we took that loss of innocent lives and multiplied it by 50, by engaging in the Second Gulf War. Did the attack on the Twin Towers accomplish anything positive? No, it resulted in a giant military buildup in the Middle East, and devastating wars in two Middle Eastern countries. Did two gulf wars accomplish our goals of eliminating terrorism? No, but it did provide a reason for a whole new generation of Americans and Middle Easterners to hate each other even more than before. War accomplishes nothing. There is only one way to completely destroy an enemy—and that is to convert that enemy into a friend, or at least a neutral party.

> This is an extremely difficult command, far from being the pious injunction of a utopian dreamer. This command is an absolute necessity for the survival of our civilization. Yes, it is love that will save our world and our civilization, love even for enemies.
>
> — *Dr. Martin Luther King Jr.*

Had we used the money that we spent on the Gulf War for charity, it would have been enough to feed, clothe, and house every person in Afghanistan and Iraq for 50 years. If the United States were the breadbasket of the world instead of the bully of the world, I can guarantee you we would be a lot more popular with the rest of the world and militarily speaking, we wouldn't need to carry such a big stick.

Make peace with the people who want to kill us? Well, I'm sure there are those who would say that this is another ridiculous utopian idea. But it's already being done on an individual basis. Phyllis and Orlando Rodriguez's 31-year-old son was killed in the terrorist attacks of September 11, 2001, but they sought peace rather than revenge. In letters to both the New York Times and President Bush, they pleaded for a solution that does not, in their words, "sink us to the inhuman level of terrorists."

The following is a section of their letter to The New York Times:

> Our son Greg is among the many missing from the World Trade Center attack. Since we first heard the news, we have shared moments of grief, comfort, hope, despair, fond memories with his wife, the two families, our friends and neighbors, his loving colleagues at Cantor Fitzgerald / Espeed, and all the grieving families that daily meet at the Pierre Hotel. We see our hurt and anger reflected among everybody we meet. We cannot pay attention to the daily flow of news about this disaster. But we read enough of the news to sense that our government is heading in the direction of violent revenge, with the prospect of sons, daughters, parents, friends in distant lands dying, suffering, and nursing further grievances against us. It is not the way to go. It will not avenge our son's death. Not in our son's name. Our son died a victim of an inhuman ideology. Our actions should not serve the same purpose. Let us grieve. Let us reflect and pray. Let us think about a rational response that brings real peace and justice to our world. But let us not as a nation add to the inhumanity of our times.[20]

In January of 2011, a week after a suicide bomber killed 21 Christians at a church in Egypt, Muslims formed human shields around Christian churches to protect them against terrorist violence. They urged cooperation and understanding between different religions, saying that we must either live together or die together. They pointed out that not all Muslims are violent, and Islam was meant to be a religion of peace and love, not violence. In countries such as Egypt, France, and Norway, Christians and Muslims are now forming cooperative groups to protect each other's religious services against terrorist threats and violence. The fact that we are learning to celebrate and respect each other's religious beliefs is a beautiful testament to humanity's ever-increasing consciousness.

> "Change comes about from millions of tiny acts that seem totally insignificant."
>
> *— Howard Zinn*

No single drop of rain has any significant power. But if it rains hard enough, it becomes an unstoppable flood. Each person must do their part to avoid violence and war. Any individual who feels led to do so can refuse to fight. Voters can refuse to support any pro-war candidate—and more importantly—each of us needs to forgive those who have harmed us and love those who have hated us. We do not have to bow to the demands of any enemy or terrorist, but we do have to change the way we view them and respond to their aggression. If we fight to defend ourselves and we defeat our enemy, and then we *celebrate* our victory, we are little better than the enemy who attacked us.

If your best friend loses his mind because of a mental illness, attacks you with a knife and forces you to defend yourself, you would not celebrate your victory in the fight. You would be sad that you had to harm your friend to defend yourself. The danger that terrorism presents to humanity lies not in the lives that the terrorists take, but rather in the fear, anguish, and hatred that we allow ourselves to feel in reaction to their decision to kill. We must forget this deceptive idea of "us versus them." This is a lie that governments, religion, and politicians promote to advance their own agendas. It has no place in our world where there is only one human race. We are all brothers and sisters and need to treat each other as such. We cannot allow our cultures to sell us the mindset of "us versus them." I am a human being first and an American second. That makes any other human being a family member, and family takes priority above country and religion. Evil dictators, communists, and terrorists are not our enemies. Our true enemies are misunderstanding, hatred, resentment, violence, and fear. These are the enemies each individual must resist by every means possible.

> As we grow in our consciousness, there will be more compassion and more love, and then the barriers between people, between religions, and between nations, will begin to fall.
>
> *— Ram Dass*

We are on the right path. Today's children are not as fanatic about war as previous generations. They want schools, hospitals, and jobs that don't involve killing or oppressing others. It is today's children who will lead our world into a new era of peace and love.

ASPECTS OF LOVE

There are a wonderful variety of pleasant emotions including kindness, gentleness, peace, security, self-control, patience, happiness, compassion, empathy, laughter, comfort, purposefulness, gratitude, curiosity, and joy. Just as every single negative emotion is an expression of fear, every single positive emotion is an expression of love. The remainder of this chapter will be dedicated to the various aspects of love as well as some ideas and scenarios that are beneficial for promoting love-based living. The more you practice love-based living here on Earth, the better prepared you will be for Heaven—a place that is ruled by love.

FORGIVE AND FORGET

Forgiveness is saying that you love and accept the other person, even though they made a mistake or did something that hurt you.

Forgiveness says *I am not going to hold anything against you. I'm going to love you just as much as I did before the incident.* Most of all, forgiveness is understanding. It is a knowing of the other person, what they felt and thought, a complete understanding that the other person's history of experiences—markedly different than yours—led them to make the decision they did, right or wrong. It is knowing and accepting that they are a flawed human being, just like you. It is saying, *When I make a mistake and I'm sorry, I want to be forgiven. So, I will do the same for you.* And even in a disagreement when you clearly have the moral high ground, reconciliation and forgiveness is still important. It is far more important to be forgiving than it is to be right.

In our culture, we are taught by TV, movies, and the media, to get revenge when someone wrongs us. What does the tough guy in the movies always do? He breaks all the rules to seek revenge and exact punishment on his enemy. No matter how many weapons are involved during the movie, in the end, it almost always ends up in a fist fight between the good guy and the bad guy. This appeals to our animal instinct to exact revenge against an enemy. But when you harm another human being, you always harm yourself because the two of you are more connected than separate. The only effective response to any resentment is forgiveness.

"I just hugged the man that murdered my son."

— Mary Johnson

Sixty-one-year-old Mary Johnson is no stranger to the concept of forgiveness. When her son's killer was released from jail after a 25-year sentence, Mary was there to forgive and embrace him. "I felt something leave me," she said. "Instantly I knew all the hatred, bitterness and animosity—I knew it was gone."[21]

Forgiveness for such atrocities is more common than one might think. The Internet is full of stories of valiant forgiveness and amazing compassion. One woman forgave the Nazis who tortured her. Another woman forgave a robber who shot her in the face. And many parents have forgiven those who killed their children. My good friend Jack struggled for years with anger and pain after his father's murder. He found the solution not in revenge, but in writing a letter of forgiveness to his father's killer as he served time in jail.

Forgiveness also makes for some very beautiful moments in life. As I was graduating high school, my parents were in the middle of a bitter divorce complete with heated arguments, a legal battle, and lots of yelling. During the next 30 years they had very little communication. But when my mother was ill and dying, my father invited her over to have Christmas dinner with the family. My father had divorced my mother and she felt very hurt and rejected, something she never really got over. I wasn't sure how the two of them would get along, but as my mother came up the front walkway, I watched my father—with a big smile on his face—welcome my mother with open arms. Seeing my parents embrace for the first time in 30 years was one of the happiest moments of my life. Forgiveness is beautiful!

Holding anger and resentment in your heart will always do more damage to you both spiritually and physically, than to the target of your resentment. If your ego is telling you that a person does not deserve to be forgiven, then do it for yourself. Forgive graciously for your own well being and happiness.

When you reach a high spiritual state, which everyone will someday, you will no longer need to forgive anyone. Each person will seem perfect in his or her own state of spiritual maturity. True love and complete understanding of another means there is nothing to forgive—there is only love. If there is somebody in your life that you have not spoken to in years because of a bitter incident between you, there is no better time like the present to make that phone call.

HONESTY

"I believe that unarmed truth and unconditional love will have the final word in reality."

— Dr. Martin Luther King, Jr.

Most dishonesty originates from selfishness and fear. The used car salesman who lies about the condition of the vehicle, and the child who lies about breaking the vase, have a common element. They both fear the reaction from the person they are lying to. Being honest, and sometimes brutally so, can be extremely difficult and unpleasant in the moment. But honesty usually works out better in the long term, especially when you develop a reputation for honesty. I still struggle with being honest, especially when it comes to revealing certain things about my life. I fear judgment from other people. Yes, being honest can result in being judged, punished, or rejected. But it is far better to be rejected for who you are than to be accepted for who you are not.

"If you tell the truth, you don't have to remember anything."

— Mark Twain

I find the more that I am honest with myself and others, the easier my life becomes. As I get older, my memory just isn't what it used to be. A poor memory is devastating for maintaining a network of lies. Such is the danger of dishonesty. Each lie requires another lie on top, and eventually the whole house of cards comes crashing down. It's better to avoid all the chaos in the first place, and just be honest from the start. If honesty is absolutely not an option, a good alternative is silence. You never have to answer a question just because somebody asks it.

SLAVERY AND FREEDOM

"You will know the truth, and the truth will set you free."

— John 8:32, NIV Bible

Living a life of anger, fear, hatred, bitterness, jealousy, and selfishness, is a life of slavery. Freedom is not about being able to go wherever you want and do whatever you want, but rather a perspective and state of mind. Freedom is the gift that the universe gives to us to reward us for letting go of our fears and embracing love. The more I let go of judgmental attitudes, prejudice, and the need to control others, the more free I feel.

Joshua Milton Blahyi was a violent warlord during the first Liberian Civil War in the 1990s. He recruited young boys to fight with him and was responsible for the deaths of over 20,000 people. Before going into battle, Joshua and his teenage troops would slaughter a young child, then eat the child's heart and drink the blood, believing it would make them brave, charge them for battle, and protect them from bullets. One day before a battle, with the blood stains from the cannibalistic ritual still on his hands, Joshua heard a voice behind him that forever changed his life. The following transcript is an interview from the TV show "Vice" on a documentary called "The Cannibal Warlords of Liberia." Joshua explains in his own words what happened:

> I heard a voice behind me say, "My son, why are you slaving?" But this was in my dialect. I looked back and I saw this man and white lady. But the light that radiated through that man was so bright that it was brighter than the sun. And I thought, I am *not* a slave, because he said, "My son, why are you slaving?" I said, "Well, in this whole territory, I am the king. I'm supposed to be a king." And he said, "You are right in saying that you are supposed to be a king. But you are living like a slave."

And those words were very hard words in my dialect. I said, "I don't understand. What are you saying?" He said, "I mean repent and live, or refuse and die." And he vanished, and the light vanished. And I came to my senses, and I was so confused. Now when I went into battle, I tried to use my pistol and it got busted. I got so afraid, I retreated from the front. I got afraid for the first time.[22]

After the incident, Joshua converted to Christianity and became the leader of an evangelic ministry headquartered in Liberia. He is now helping to convert to Christianity many of the same children who fought along side him in the war. Direct intervention from Heaven transformed the former general from the slavery of war to the freedom of love.

PATIENCE

"Patience is not just about waiting for something... it's about how you wait, or your attitude while waiting."

— *Joyce Meyer*

So many people spend their lives fretting about yesterday and worrying about tomorrow, but this is not how human beings were meant to live. We are happiest and thrive when we choose to live in the present moment. When a person is impatient, it essentially means they are not happy with the present moment and want it to change as soon as possible. Having patience with others is a wonderful display of love. It shows that you understand that each person does things at their own pace, and you accept the pace at which others operate. Being patient means recognizing that you are immortal and that you literally have all of eternity to do the things you want. You can slow down and relax. You never have to be in a hurry. You can choose to live in the moment and accept every situation as it is.

An excellent place to practice patience is while driving. I like to leave myself lots of extra time whenever I drive anywhere, because it's a lot easier to be patient with other drivers when I am not in a hurry. I can always tell if I'm in the right frame of mind spiritually by driving during rush hour traffic. When I have the proper attitude, I actually *like* being in traffic. Where else can I show patience, peace, and kindness to total strangers for hours at a time? And if there ever were a place that desperately needs more patience, it is on the road. When you master patience, you will be a shining light and an example to others. Having patience with both yourself and others is a critical element to living in a state of peace.

PEACE

One major expression of love is peace, which comes when we release fear. Peace comes from simply knowing that long term we are taken care of and protected. Just like so many other aspects of love, peace is not a set of circumstances. It is perceiving the world with a full understanding of who you are and trusting that you are always cared for and protected even when your intellect tells you otherwise. Peace is also trusting, no matter how bad the situation is, that in the end, any suffering is but the blink of an eye in this physical plane. The truth about God is that he understands the big picture, but we do not. We aren't qualified from a perspective of wisdom to experience justifiable fear. We don't understand our situation well enough to assess that we are in any real danger, because any and all danger is perceived only from an earthly perspective. In reality, we are powerful beings of light and energy, indestructible and immortal. Nothing can harm us in the long-term. Absolutely nothing. There is nothing to fear, not even fear itself.

GIFTING

We are born into this world with absolutely no physical possessions—and when we die, we leave the same way. We're not so much owners of the things we have, but temporary managers. Money is in our hands for a short time, and then it is left for the next person. Knowing that we are managers of wealth and not owners, makes it easier to be generous. Sharing when we are able is a great way to show love to each other.

Tipping is an excellent way to express gratitude and love. It is an opportunity to be generous with a stranger that you know will accept the gift without thinking you have any ulterior motives. It's not so much the money that really matters, but the fact that it is saying to the person "I appreciate you, and I'm grateful for your contribution of labor to help meet my needs."

It is important, when you are offered a gift, to accept it with gratitude—no matter how much guilt you may feel in the moment. If you refuse a gift from another person you deny yourself the pleasure of receiving a gift, and you deny the other person an opportunity to grow their soul. But if you accept the gift, everybody wins. The person giving the gift experiences growth in their soul from their loving act of generosity, and the person receiving the gift is changed by the act of love from the giver. The good vibrations between the two will resonate through the entire Earth and elevate all of humanity.

Gifting is also an excellent way to achieve success. True success has nothing to do with how much money a person makes or how much wealth they have accumulated. It has everything to do with how they treat the people around them. Give from your heart when you feel led, never out of obligation, but only out of true desire and compassion.

TALK TO STRANGERS

Most people naturally treat family members and friends far better than they treat strangers. We are taught from a young age not to trust strangers. If I have no friendship or rapport built up, why should I be kind to a stranger? What's in it for me? That is generally the backwards thinking that our culture has programmed into our minds since childhood. But believe it or not, at a soul level, you know every person on Earth intimately. They are all part of your very close-knit family of light. Knowing this, it is best not to mistreat any stranger. A good guideline is, if you wouldn't treat your best friend or your mother that way, you probably shouldn't be treating a stranger that way.

If you were at a red light and your mother was in front of you texting on her cell phone when the light turned green, you wouldn't lay on your horn and curse at her, would you? You would probably tap on the horn gently to let her know the light was green, and you might even be slightly annoyed. But you probably wouldn't really let it upset you or anger you because it's your mother. Let me assure you that every person on Earth is connected to you and is just as important as your own mother.

If your brother was a heroin addict living on the street and asked you for spare change, you probably would not give it to him. That's because you wouldn't want him to harm himself by taking more heroin. That's okay. That is true love expressed in the best way you can. But alternatively, you might offer to buy him a meal or give him a change of clothes. We have to treat each person on Earth as if they were our brother or sister, because they are. It is only a state of temporary amnesia that conceals this reality.

A SIMPLE ACT OF LOVE

> "Let us always meet each other with a smile, for a smile is the beginning of love."

> — *Mother Teresa*

When I go out in public and walk down the street it makes me so sad to see the faces of people who are hurried, stressed, depressed, or suffering. Sometimes, they don't even want to look me in the eyes when they pass by. When I see one of my brothers or sisters that I've never met before and may never see again—I like to smile. It lets them know I care about them and accept them without knowing them personally. Yes, sometimes a person will misinterpret my smile as flirtation, but that's okay. That's just a strange reaction that our culture has taught us. It is still important for me to smile as much as I can. A smile lets the world know that I'm happy, and I want others to be happy too. It tells others *you don't have to be afraid of me; I'm a good person and I am safe*. A smile is one of the most wonderful acts of love that one stranger can show to another. When you smile, you are opening the essence of your soul. I try and use smiling as much as possible. Sometimes I'm in a bad mood and I just don't feel like smiling, and that's okay too. But I like myself best when I do smile at others. It makes me feel good, and I know from the reactions I get that it, more often than not, makes others feel good too. I encourage everyone reading this book to give it a try and smile at others as much as possible. It's amazing how such a small thing can change your day and add a little brightness to the lives of others who often feel lonely from the cold indifference so prevalent in our modern society.

GREETING PEOPLE

You may have had the experience of seeing someone that you haven't seen in a long time and gotten a semi-cold reception—sort of a nonchalant acknowledgement. It feels pretty lousy, doesn't it? But I'm sure you have experienced the opposite. You see someone that you haven't seen in awhile, and with a big smile and open arms, they greet you because they are genuinely happy to see you. Such a greeting feels so much better because the other person is saying with the way they greeted you, "I missed you and I am very happy to see you."

The way we greet each other is *so* important. When appropriate, I encourage people to be as free with their smiles and hugs as much as possible.

THE POWER OF LOVE: HUGS AND CUDDLES HAVE LONG-TERM EFFECTS

How often do you hug? Do you like to sit close and hold each other's hands? Recent research shows it's good for your health. Between loving partners, between parents and children, or even between close friends, physical affection can help the brain, the heart and other body systems you might never have imagined.

At the center of how our bodies respond to love and affection is a hormone called oxytocin. Most of our oxytocin is made in the area of the brain called the hypothalamus. Some is released into our bloodstream, but much of its effect is thought to reside in the brain.

Oxytocin makes us feel good when we're close to family and other loved ones, including pets. It does this by acting through what scientists call the *dopamine reward system*. Dopamine is a brain chemical that plays a crucial part in how we perceive pleasure.

Oxytocin does more than make us feel good. It lowers the levels of stress hormones in the body, reducing blood pressure, improving mood, increasing tolerance for pain, and perhaps even speeding how fast wounds heal. It also seems to play an important role in our relationships. It's been linked, for example, to how much we trust others.

We may not yet fully understand how love and affection develop between people—or how love affects our health—but research is giving us some guidance. Give those you love all the affection you can. It can't hurt, and it may bring a bounty of health benefits.[23]

GOD'S LOVE FOR US

How much does God love us? We see God as perfect: And he sees us the same way! God sees us in the same manner that we might perceive a young child. The child is not mature, nor wise, and makes many mistakes. And the young child is not very useful for performing many productive tasks. But with all of a child's flaws and shortcomings, he is so perfect and adorable just the way he is. And in just the same way that we see that beautiful, innocent young child, God sees us as perfect and wonderful. You never have to doubt God's love for you. He *has* to love you because you are part of him, and he is part of you. You and God are *more* than family.

ADVICE ON LIVING LOVE:

Love, in whatever form and in whatever manner it is expressed, is the vital element to our happiness on earth. Loving any hobby, activity, or even any ideal will not provide fulfillment and happiness to human beings. What we need is love for each other. Money, power, social status, and material possessions will not replace what we get from loving and being loved by another.

There is no greater love than the love that we share for each other. This is the only true love.

— *Lia Shapiro, author*
and new age mystic

People are often unreasonable, irrational, and self-centered; forgive them anyway. If you are kind, people may accuse you of selfish, ulterior motives; be kind anyway. If you are successful, you will win some unfaithful friends and some genuine enemies; succeed anyway. If you are honest and sincere, people may deceive you; be honest and sincere anyway. What you spend years creating, others could destroy overnight; create anyway. If you find serenity and happiness, some may be jealous; be happy anyway. The good you do today will often be forgotten; do good anyway. Give the best you have, and it will never be enough; give your best anyway. In the final analysis, it is between you and God. It was never between you and them anyway.

— *Mother Teresa*
(adapted from Dr. Kent Keith)

Seek to live as clean a life as possible! When in doubt, ask Heaven to show you how. Always try to do what you deeply believe to be the right thing. Be as loving and generous to others as possible. Seek to be grace oriented and forgiving of others' weaknesses. However, know that you need not be a pawn or a fool to anyone's vanity or manipulation. Pray for and send wishes of Love and Light to those who hurt you or those you disagree with. Practice self-control and self-discipline, especially in the face of what you know is not for your higher good. Remind yourself that living a life in the light is much more beneficial and gratifying long-term than a few measly moments of "dark" fun. Speak to God often and give thanks when you wake up every morning and before you go to bed. Every good parent likes to hear loving words from his or her child. Make sure you express words of love and praise to your Heavenly parent. Make sure you show appreciation toward the kindness of others. And make sure you are being loving and honest, regardless of how others may treat you. Avoiding what your spirit tells you is evil will keep you and your home empowered and attract toward you those who are filled with light and good energy. Joy-filled laughter that is not at someone else's expense is always excellent medicine.

> — *Christian Andreson,*
> *spiritual counselor*

To say that I am made in the image of God is to say that love is the reason for my existence, for God is love. Love is my true identity. Selflessness is my true self. Love is my true character. Love is my name.

> — *Thomas Merton, author and poet*

If only we could realize while we are yet mortals, that day by day we are building for eternity, how different our lives in many ways would be! Every gentle word, every generous thought, every unselfish deed, will become a pillar of eternal beauty in the life to come. We cannot be selfish and unloving in one life and generous and loving in the next. The two lives are too closely blended. One is but a continuation of the other.

— Rebecca Ruter Springer, author

THE POWER OF LOVE

Unconditional love is the purest form of pleasure. There is no greater joy, no greater feeling of fulfillment and oneness. The love in your soul is far more powerful than your mind can comprehend. Given enough love, there is no problem that can't be untangled. In order to give love, you must first find it in yourself. So, love yourself, then open yourself to the love of others. Every human being is a beautiful expression of God's creation, regardless of their decisions to act in light or darkness, so love people for who they are, not for who you want them to be. Love as much as you can, by all means you can, in all ways you can, in all places you can, at all times you can, to all people you can, and for as long as you can. Living in unconditional love is so easy that even a child can do it, and they do.

CLOSING PRAYER

During my 55 years of life, I've seen many beautiful places and had many great adventures. I have climbed the stairs of the Eiffel Tower, walked inside the colosseum in Rome, bungee jumped off the Stratosphere Tower in Las Vegas, hang glided over the Rocky Mountains of California, skydived over the Mojave Desert, traveled through the jungles of Central America, and scuba dived with whales in Australia's Great Barrier Reef. But my greatest, most beautiful, and most exciting adventure by far has been my spiritual journey. It takes no money, and anyone can do it. Go and have your adventure! Live, play, laugh, learn, spread joy, and love in all circumstances. My hope and prayer for you was summed up beautifully over 800 years ago by Saint Francis of Assisi's prayer:

> Lord, make me an instrument of your peace. Where there is hatred, let me sow love; where there is injury, pardon; where there is doubt, faith; where there is despair, hope; where there is darkness, light; and where there is sadness, joy. O Divine Master, grant that I may not so much seek to be consoled as to console; to be understood as to understand; to be loved as to love. For it is in giving that we receive; it is in pardoning that we are pardoned; and it is in dying that we are born to eternal life. Amen.

ENDNOTES

Dr. Maurice Rawlings, "To Hell and Back," (Trinity Broadcasting Network, 1999,) VHS.

Rawlings, "To Hell"

Kate Broome, "The Day I Died" (BBC, 2002,) TV Release.

Liz Dale, Ph.D., "Crossing Over & Coming Home" (Emerald Ink Publishing, 2008), p 57.

Rawlings, "To Hell"

Rawlings, "To Hell"

Rawlings, "To Hell"

Marvin J. Bestman, "My Journey to Heaven" (Baker Publishing Group, 2012)

Dr. Dianne Morrissey, "International Association for Near-death Studies (IANDS)" http://www.near-death.com/resources/quotes.html

Piper, Don and Murphey, Cecil. "90 Minutes In Heaven" (Baker Publishing Group, 2015) p. 29-33

Bestman, "My Journey"

Broome, "The Day I Died"

Peter Shockey, "Life After Life" (Documentary, 1992)

Vol 37, Issue 34, "The Onion News" (September 26, 2001)

Kryon (Lee Carroll) "The Recalibration of Belief" YouTube Video https://www.youtube.com/watch?v=i7wHb8pmXyc

Kryon (Lee Carroll)

The Daily Express (Trinidad Express Newspapers) "The Last One Out" (Jan. 20, 2012) http://www.trinidadexpress.com/woman-magazine/THE_LAST__ONE_OUT-137804728.html

"Bashar's (Darryl Anka) Most Profound Speech" YouTube Video https://www.youtube.com/watch?v=G5DX337IO7A

Raoul Martinez, "Creating Freedom: The Lottery of Birth" (Documentary, 2013)

"In Our Son's Name" http://www.inoursonsname.com

National Public Radio "Forgiving Her Son's Killer: 'Not an Easy Thing'" http://www.npr.org/2011/05/20/136463363/forgiving-her-sons-killer-not-an-easy-thing

Vice, "The Cannibal Warlords of Liberia (Full Length Documentary)" YouTube video, https://www.youtube.com/watch?v=ZRuSS0iiFyo

News in Health, "The Power of Love: Hugs and Cuddles Have Long-Term Effects" (February 2007) https://newsinhealth.nih.gov/2007/February/docs/01features_01.htm

BIBLIOGRAPHY

Bardo Thodol (The Tibetan Book of the Dead) ~ 750 A.D.

Bestman, Marvin J. *My Journey to Heaven: What I Saw and How It Changed My Life*, Baker Publishing Group, 2012

Brinkley, Dannion. *Saved by The Light*, New York: Villard Books, 1994

Copernicus, Nicolaus. *De Revolutionibus Orbium Coelestium (On the Revolutions of the Celestial Spheres,)* Nuremberg: Johannes Petreius, 1543

Dale, Liz, Ph.D. *Crossing Over & Coming Home*, Hot Springs: Emerald Ink Publishing, 2008

Eadie, Betty J. *Embraced by The Light*, Gold Leaf Press, 1992

Fenimore, Angie. *Beyond the Darkness*, Bantam Books, 1995

Gibson, Arvin S. *Journeys Beyond Life*, Horizon Publishers, 1994

Jordan, Kathie. *The Birth Called Death*, RiverWood Books, 2003

Lerma M.D., John. *Into the Light*, New Page Books, 2007

Luckett, D.C., Mary Ann. *An Answer From Heaven*, For Them, 2009

Moody, Jr., M.D., Raymond A. *Life After Life*, HarperCollins Publishers, 1975

Richie, George G. *Return from Tomorrow*, Baker Publishing Group, 1978

Rives, Kim. *My Walk Thru Heaven*, 2008

Springer, Recbecca Ruter. *My Dream of Heaven* (Intra Muros), Harrison House, 2002

Storm, Howard. *My Descent Into Death: A Second Chance at Life*, Harmony, 2005

Temple, Eric. *With One Voice*, The Forest Way, 2009

Wise, Bill. *23 Minutes in Hell*, Charisma House, 2006

Wood, Dr. Gary. *A Place Called Heaven*, Gary Wood Ministries, 2002

ABOUT THE AUTHOR

David Suich is a retired engineer who founded and operated Steps of Hope Outreach, a nonprofit organization that served orphanages in Nepal, Mexico, and Haiti from 2003 through 2018. During a painful and chronic physical condition that triggered severe depression, he clicked on a YouTube video about an atheist who died momentarily and saw Heaven. This lead him on a 12-year journey of research into near death experiences including the testimonies of over 700 people who have died, seen the afterlife, and returned.

Printed in the USA
CPSIA information can be obtained
at www.ICGtesting.com
LVHW040043010823
753622LV00002B/411